CHARACTERISTICS OF THE
MILDLY HANDICAPPED

CHARACTERISTICS OF THE MILDLY HANDICAPPED

Assisting Teachers, Counselors, Psychologists
and Families to Prepare for Their Roles
in Meeting the Needs of the Mildly Handicapped
in a Changing Society

By

HAROLD D. LOVE, ED.D.

Professor, Special Education
University of Central Arkansas

C H A R L E S   C   T H O M A S   •   P U B L I S H E R ,   L T D.
Springfield • Illinois • U.S.A.

Published and Distributed Throughout the World by

CHARLES C THOMAS • PUBLISHER, LTD.
2600 South First Street
Springfield, Illinois 62794-9265

ISBN 0-398-06713-9   (cloth)
ISBN 0-398-06714-7   (paper)
Library of Congress Catalog Card Number: 96-28214

With THOMAS BOOKS *careful attention is given to all details of manufacturing
and design. It is the Publisher's desire to present books that are satisfactory as to their
physical qualities and artistic possibilities and appropriate for their particular use.*
THOMAS BOOKS *will be true to those laws of quality that assure a good name
and good will.*

Printed in the United States of America
SC-R-3

Library of Congress Cataloging-in-Publication Data

Love, Harold D.
    Characteristics of the mildly handicapped : assisting teachers,
counselors, psychologists, and families to prepare for their roles
in meeting the needs of the mildly handicapped in a changing society
/ by Harold D. Love.
      p.   cm.
    Includes bibliographical references and indexes.
    ISBN 0-398-06713-9.— ISBN 0-398-06714-7 (pbk.)
    1. Handicapped children—Education—United States.
2. Developmental disabilities—United States.   3. Learning
disabilities—United States.   I. Title.
LC4031.L67   1997
371.92'82—dc20
                                              96-28214
                                               CIP

To my wife
Sue McDavid Love
And to my children
Hal, Laina, Susie, and Wendy
I dedicate this book.

PREFACE

Practically all school teachers can expect to encounter exceptional children in their classrooms. There has been a marked decrease in institutionalization of exceptional individuals and implementation of mainstreaming. This book is about the mildly handicapped who are always found in the regular classroom but who spend some time in the resource room for special attention in reading, math, English, etc.

The special needs of the mildly handicapped have become the shared responsibility of regular education teachers, counselors, psychologists, and other members of the education team, including parents and families of the mildly handicapped. This text is intended to assist in the preparation of those individuals for their roles in meeting the needs of the mildly handicapped in a changing society.

I am indebted to Mrs. Jean Thompson for typing, editing, and helping in many ways in the making of this book.

To those professors who choose this book for adoption and to those students who will use it as an information source on people with differences I hope this text meets their expectations.

This book is about the largest group of learning disabled children and youth served in the public schools of America, the mildly handicapped, and the teachers and service personnel who work with them.

Harold D. Love

CONTENTS

CHARACTERISTICS OF THE MILDLY HANDICAPPED

Chapter 1

EXCEPTIONALITY AND SPECIAL EDUCATION

Gerald is eleven years old and in the sixth grade at Greenville Middle School. In reading, writing, and arithmetic, Gerald's performance is typical for a boy of eleven years of age. Achievement test scores indicate that Gerald is at the middle sixth grade level in all subject areas. It is the beginning of the second semester and he recently took an IQ test which indicated an intelligence quotient of 105. Gerald is athletic, has 20/20 vision, and no measurable hearing loss. He has no serious medical problems. He has developed emotionally at a level commensurate with his chronological age. He gets along well with family and peers. Is Gerald normal? Gerald meets the basic criteria for normalcy. But what is normal and how do we determine the criteria for normalcy?

In any given culture, *normal* is a relative term. Also, what is normal in one culture may not be in another. What is normal in a subculture such as a gang may not be normal elsewhere in the country. *Normal*, therefore, is a relative term and defined in the context of a culture. There are, however, people who do not meet the criteria of *normalcy* as defined by our culture. They may be physically, mentally, or emotionally different from other people in our society. Every person is different from every other person in some way. Therefore, the type and extent of the differences become important. Every society creates descriptions to identify these differences.

Who Is the Exceptional Child?

Many people in education have attempted to define the exceptional child. Some use it to define any atypical child. Others use it to define the mentally retarded or the exceptionally bright child. Kirk, Gallagher, and Anastasiow (1993) define the exceptional child as:

A child who differs from the average or normal child in (1) mental characteristics, (2) sensory abilities, (3) communication abilities, (4) behavior and emotional development, or (5) physical characteristics. These differences must occur to such

3

an extent that the child requires a modification of school practices, or special education services, to develop his or her unique capabilities.

Characteristics of Exceptional Children

Many children are exceptional if we describe them as differing from the group norm. A boy is exceptional if he goes to a school where all the other children are girls. A child with red hair is exceptional if he is in a class with children having blond, black, and brown hair. However, educationally speaking, the boy in the class of girls is not exceptional if we do not have to modify the curriculum for him. In education, we group children for various reasons. Kirk, Gallagher, and Anastasiow (1993) tell us that the following groupings are typical:

1. Intellectual differences, including children who are intellectually superior and children who are slow to learn
2. Communication differences, including children with learning disabilities or speech and language impairments
3. Sensory differences, including children with auditory or visual impairments
4. Behavioral differences, including children who are emotionally disturbed or socially maladjusted
5. Multiple and severe handicapping conditions, including children with combinations of impairments (cerebral palsy and mental retardation; deafness and blindness)
6. Physical differences, including children with nonsensory disabilities that impede mobility and physical vitality.

Over the years the gifted and talented child has been revered and held in high esteem. The mentally and physically handicapped have not been so lucky. Change has been slow in bringing down the barriers of discrimination for this type child in school, the work place, and in society in general.

Legal Reform

During the past three decades there have been several court cases which helped the handicapped overcome barriers placed before them by society.

The court cases and federal legislation listed in Table 1.1 focused on the rights for the handicapped.

The Americans With Disabilities Act of 1990

On July 26, 1990, President George Bush signed into law a sweeping civil rights legislation act: The Americans with Disabilities Act (ADA) (Public Law 101-336). The legislation defines a person with a disability

Table 1.1
Major Court Cases and Federal Legislation Focusing
on the Right of Individuals Who Are Handicapped.

Court Cases and Federal Legislation	Precedents Established
Brown v. Topeka, Kansas Board of Education (1954)	Segregation of students by race held unconstitutional. Education is a right that must be available to all on equal terms.
Hobsen v. Hansen (1960)	The doctrine of equal educational opportunity is a part of the law of due process, and denying an equal educational opportunity is a violation of the Constitution.
Diana v. California State Board of Education (1970)	Children tested for potential placement in a special education program must be assessed in their native or primary language. Children cannot be placed in special classes on the basis of culturally biased tests.
Pennsylvania Association of Retarded Citizens v. Commonwealth of Pennsylvania (1971	Pennsylvania schools must provide a free public education to all school-age retarded children.
Mills v. Board of Education of the Disctict of Columbia (1972)	Declared exclusion of individuals with disabilities from free, appropriate public education is a violation of the due-process and equal protection clauses of the Fourteenth Amendment to the Constitution. Public schools in the District of Columbia must provide a free education to all children with disabilities regardless of their functional level or ability to adapt to the present educational system.
Public Law 93-112, Vocational Rehabilitation Act of 1973, Section 504 (1973)	Individuals with disabilities cannot be excluded from participation in, denied benefits of, or subjected to discrimination under any program or activity receiving federal financial assistance.
Public Law 93-380, Educational Amendments Act (1974)	Financial aid was provided to the states for implementation of programs for children who are exceptional, including the gifted and talented. Due-process requirements (procedural safeguards) were established to protect the rights of children with disabilities and their families in special education placement decisions.
Public Law 94-142, Part B of the Education of the Handicapped Act (1975)	A free and appropriate public education must be provided for all children with disabilities in the United States. (Those up to 5 years old may be excluded in some states.)
Public Law 99-457, Education of the Handicapped Act amendments (1986)	A new authority extended free and appropriate education to all children with disabilities ages 3 to 5 and provided a new early intervention program for infants and toddlers.
Public Law 99-372, Handicapped Children's Protection Act (1986)	Reimbursement of attorney's fees and expenses was given to parents who prevail in administrative proceedings or court actions.
Public Law 101-336, Americans with Disabilities Act (1990)	Civil rights protections were provided for people with disabilities in private-sector employment, all public services, and public accommodations, transportation and telecommunications.
Public Law 101-476, Individuals with Disabilities Education Act (1990)	The Education of the Handicapped Act amendments were renamed the Individuals with Disabilities Education Act (IDEA). Two new categories of disability were added; autism and traumatic brain injury. IDEA requires that an individualized transition plan be developed no later than age 16 as a component of the IEP process. Rehabilitation and social work services are included as related services.

as (1) having a physical or mental impairment that substantially limits him/her in some major life activity and (2) having experienced discrimination resulting from this physical or mental impairment. ADA charged the federal government with the task of ensuring that these provisions be enforced on behalf of all people with disabilities (West, 1991).

The information about ADA in Table 1.2 may prove to be of interest to the reader.

Table 1.2
The Americans with Disabilities Act of 1990: Breaking Down the Barriers

Did you know that, in public and private employment . . . ?	Did you know that, in public accommodations . . . ?
- Employers cannot discriminate against an individual with a disability in hiring or promotion if the person is otherwise qualified for the job. - Employers can ask about someone's ability to perform a job but cannot inquire if he or she has a disability or subject him or her to tests that tend to screen out people with disabilities. - Employers need to provide reasonable accommodation to people with disabilities, such as job restructuring and modification of equipment.	- Restaurants, hotels, and retail stores may not discriminate against individuals with disabilities. - Physical barriers in existing facilities must be removed, if removal is readily achievable. If not, alternative methods of providing the services must be offered. - All new construction and alterations of facilities must be accessible.
Did you know that in public transportation . . . ?	Did you know that, in government . . . ?
- New public transit buses, bus and train stations, and rail systems must be accessible to individuals with disabilities. - Transit authorities must provide transportation services to individuals with disabilities who cannot use fixed-route bus services. - All Amtrak stations must be accessible to people with disabilities by the year 2010.	- State and local agencies may not discriminate against qualified individuals with disabilities. - All government facilities, services, and communications must be accessible to people with disabilities.
	Did you know that, in telecommunications . . . ?
	- Companies offering telephone service to the general public must offer telephone relay services to individuals who use telecommunication devices for the deaf or similar devices.

History of Special Education

During the last century, we have seen tremendous changes in the way society treats exceptional children. This country has moved from a social posture of rejection and isolation of children with disabilities to the acceptance of these children as contributing members of society. In the political forum, we honor certain founders of our country: Washington, Jefferson, Madison, Franklin, Adams, and others. These men are long dead, but we still recognize that their ideas, their perseverence, and their values helped shape society the way it is today. In special education, there are a number of pioneering people who influence the field even today. The concepts of intelligence developed by Alfred Binet, and later, Lewis Terman and David Wechsler, are still in use today. The system developed by Louis Braille when he was only 15 years of age is still in use today. The works of Edward Seguin and Maria Montessori in their educational exercises are still in existence today. Above all, the works of Samuel Gridley Howe and Alexander Graham Bell, along with Dorthea Dix and their beliefs that children need more than custodial care is still a driving factor in special education today.

As we look back in history, we find that the concept of educating every child to his or her greatest potential is a relatively new idea. As a matter of fact, although the first special class in public schools came about in Boston in 1869, the concept of educating every child to his potential has really come about in the last thirty years. The current use of the term *exceptional* is itself a reflection of a tremendous change in society's view of people who differ from the norm. The world has come a long way from the Spartan practice of murdering physically handicapped children and infants, but the journey has been a slow one, moving from the asylum to the institution to the mainstream in education. It probably started in 1799 when a wild boy was found roaming in the forest of Aveyron in the south of France and Jean Marc Gaspard Itard decided that he would educate this wild boy. A noted psychiatrist of that day, whose name was Pinel, diagnosed the boy as an idiot and Itard undertook the task of educating this boy he had named Victor. Although he worked with the boy on a daily basis for approximately five years, he taught him very little. Itard did keep elaborate notes, though, on his training methods which he later published, and we still use some of Itard's methods in teaching special education and regular education today.

The work of Thomas Hopkins Gallaudet, who became interested in teaching the deaf when he was tutoring the child of an American physician, is a monument to the education of the deaf. Gallaudet went to Europe and studied deaf education in Paris, France under a man named Abbe de l'Epee who had founded a school. Abbe de l'Eppe used the manual approach for teaching the deaf and that is why when Thomas Hopkins Gallaudet came back to America and established the first school for the deaf we had the manual approach.

Samuel Gridley Howe was born in 1801 and died in 1876. This American believed that children with disabilities can learn and should have an organized education, not just compassionate care. Samuel Gridley Howe not only helped establish numerous institutions for the mentally retarded, but he was also the first director of the Perkin's Institute for the Blind in Watertown, Massachusetts.

Louis Braille was born in 1809 and died in 1852. This French boy was blinded in a home accident when he was approximately three years of age and was then sent to an institution. Louis Braille devised an alternative system of communication based on a code of raised dots. This was first published when Louis Braille was only 15 years old and it is now used around the world.

Edward Seguin, another Frenchman, was born in 1812 and died in 1880. He believed that children who are mentally retarded can learn if taught through specific sensory-motor exercises. Edward Seguin came to America when things became politically difficult for him to remain in France and he was instrumental in founding several institutions for the mentally retarded. He also had a hand in forming the American Association on Mental Deficiency which is now known as the American Association on Mental Retardation. Edward Seguin always insisted that every institution founded by him and his cohorts have a unit for the education of the retarded.

In 1822, Francis Galton, an Englishman, was born. He is not only known as the father of testing, but also, he believed that genius tends to run in families and its origin can be determined. Francis Galton determined that genius is inherited by tracing family trees and proving that genius crops up regularly in every family where there is genius. He published two books on this subject.

Alexander Graham Bell has already been mentioned, but this American was born in 1847 and believed that children who have a hearing disability can learn to speak and can use their limited hearing if it is amplified. Alexander Graham Bell also went to Europe and studied the oral approach for teaching the deaf and brought it back to America along with Samuel Gridley Howe and established the first school for teaching deaf children using the oral approach.

Alfred Binet's name has already been mentioned for establishing the first intelligence test that could measure cognitive ability. Binet published this, along with his associates, Simon and Henri. His test was later standardized in the United States by Henry Goddard and then later standardized again by Lewis Terman which later became the Stanford-Binet. For several years, the Stanford-Binet was the only good intelligence test that we had in America.

Maria Montessori, an Italian woman born in 1870, believed that children can learn at a very early age, using concrete experiences designed around special instructional material. Maria Montessori also worked with children in the slums as well as children who were classified as being emotionally disturbed. She used the tracing method for the teaching of reading long before Grace Fernald, Helen Keller, or any of the other people who claim credit for the method.

Alfred Strauss, a German born in 1897, who immigrated to America, believed that some children show unique patterns of learning disabilities, probably from brain injury, and that these children require special training. Alfred Strauss and Laura Lehtinen developed methods for teaching children who were then called brain injured. Today, we call them children having specific learning disabilities.

Anna Freud, an Austrian woman born in 1895, believed that the techniques of psychoanalysis can be applied to children who have emotional problems. Much of the work of Anna Freud is still used in treating emotionally disturbed children today.

Establishing Schools

Nineteenth-century reformers such as Horace Mann, Samuel Gridley Howe, and Dorthea Dix gave impetus to the establishment of residential institutions. Beginning in 1817 to approximately 1865, a span of more than forty years, many states established residential schools for children who were deaf, blind, mentally retarded, or orphaned. These residential schools were patterned after similar schools in Europe. In 1817, the American Asylum for the Education and Instruction of the Deaf, a residential institution, was opened in Hartford, Connecticut. Today, it is called the American School for the Deaf. In 1829, The New England

Asylum for the Blind was opened and this school was later renamed the Perkins School for the Blind after the man who gave them the land on which to build it in Watertown, Massachusetts. Thirty years later, a residential school for the mentally retarded, the Massachusetts School for Idiots and Feeble Minded Youth, was established in South Boston. If one reads the history of special education, he or she will see that Massachusetts was at the cutting edge of many aspects of the education of exceptional children. The school in South Boston is now called the Fernald State School for the Mentally Retarded.

Table 1.3 lists some of the major contributors to the field of special education. The present shape of special education is difficult to understand without a sense of those whose contributions changed the face of education during their time which, naturally, extended into the future.

Special Education Today

During the past several years, a number of national studies have attempted to provide us with a clearer picture of the state of special education in the United States. Who is being served and what does it take to serve them? Later in this chapter the reader will see who is being served in special education.

Wagner, D'Amico et al. (1991) indicate that the following factors influence whether a student drops out or stays in school:

- Only 5% of students who were absent 10 days or less dropped out.
- Over 10% of students who were absent 21 to 30 days dropped out.
- Almost 27% of those absent more than 30 days dropped out.
- Students who failed one or more courses dropped out at a rate of 17%; those who passed all their courses had a dropout rate of almost 6%.
- Students with high absenteeism and those who fail a class do not often develop a social bond with their schools, or identify their classes as relevant or interesting.
- Students with disabilities who received job-specific vocational education performed better in school and at work than those who did not, had significantly lower absenteeism, and were significantly less likely than others to have dropped out of school.
- Students who received individual attention such as tutoring or counseling were more likely to stay in school.
- Students who socialized with other students outside of school and were involved in extracurricular activities were less likely to fail a course, miss school, or drop out.
- Smaller classes, tutoring, and other services increased the chances that students with disabilities would succeed in general classes.
- Students with disabilities in general classes were less likely to have high

Table 1.3
Major Ideas Influencing Special Education in the United States

Initiator	Dates	Major Idea
Jean Marc Itard	1775-1838	Single-subject research can be used to develop training methods for those who are mentally retarded.
Thomas Hopkins Gallaudet	1787-1851	Children who are deaf can learn to communicate by spelling and gesturing with their fingers.
Samuel Gridley Howe	1801-1876	Children with disabilities can learn and should have an organized education, not just compassionate care.
Louis Braille	1809-1852	Children who are blind can learn through an alternative system of communication.
Edward Seguin	1812-1880	Children who are mentally retarded can learn if taught through specific sensory-motor exercises.
Francis Galton	1822-1911	Genius tends to run in families, and its origin can be determined.
Alexander Graham Bell	1847-1911	Children who have a hearing disability can learn to speak, and can use their limited hearing if it is amplified.
Alfred Binet	1857-1911	Intelligence can be measured, and it can be improved through education.
Maria Montesorri	1870-1952	Children can learn at very early ages, using concrete experiences designed around special instructional materials.
Lewis Terman	1877-1956	Intelligence tests can be used to identify gifted children, who tend to maintain superiority throughout life.
Anna Freud	1895-1982	The techniques of psychoanalysis can be applied to children who have emotional problems.
Alfred Strauss	1897-1957	Some children show unique patterns of learning disabilities, probably from brain injury, that require special training.

absenteeism or to be retained in grade if classes were small or if they had help from an instructional aide.

- Students with more serious disabilities were often "encouraged" by school administrators to drop out.

Table 1.4 shows a breakdown of the projection of racial/ethnic categories receiving services in 1990.

Table 1.4
Projected 1990 Racial/Ethnic Breakdown of Students
Receiving Special Education Under Selected Categories

	Native American	Asian	Hispanic	African American	Total Minority	Total White
Percentage of All Students in School	1%	3%	12%	16%	32%	68%
Disability Category						
Mental Retardation	1	1	11	34	47	53
Speech Impairments	1	2	9	16	27	73
Serious Emotional Disturbance	1	1	6	22	29	71
Specific Learning Disabilities	1	1	11	17	30	70

Haselkorn and Calkins (1993) tell us that of the 45 teaching areas, the four with the highest need and most considerable shortage are special education areas: Multiple Disabilities, Emotional/Behavioral Disorders, Learning Disabilities, and Speech Pathology/Audiology.

The U.S. Department of Education, National Center for Education Statistics (1978–93) has this to say about special education:

- Of the 608,504 personnel employed to provide for the education of students with disabilities, only 17,373 (2.9%) are local supervisors or administrators.
- The average teacher/pupil ratio in self-contained programs range from 1:13 for learning disabilities programs to 1:14 for programs serving students with hearing impairments, with an average ratio and average class size of 9 students.
- The average caseload for resource programs is 26 students, ranging from 10 students in mental retardation and visual impairment programs to 50 in programs for students with speech/language disabilities.
- Compared to general education teachers, special education teachers are statistically more likely to be female, younger, unmarried, have fewer years of teaching experience, and have earned a master's degree.

Who Completes School and Who Leaves

Figure 1.1 indicates the special education category of students who completed school through the category with the least years in school.

How Much Is Spent on Special Education

Moore (1988) says that while no data are collected on the total amount of money expended to educate students with disabilities, it is possible to

Who completes school and who leaves?

	COMPLETED SCHOOL	DID NOT COMPLETE SCHOOL

Learning Disabilities . . . . 63.9% / 36.1%

Serious Emotional Disturbance . . . . 45.2% / 54.8%

Speech Impairments . . . . 67.5% / 32.5%

Mental Retardation . . . . 66.4% / 33.6%

Visual Impairments . . . . 83.2% / 16.8%

Hearing Impairments . . . . 84.5% / 15.5%

Deaf . . . . 88.2% / 11.8%

Orthopedic Impairments . . . . 83.0% / 17.0%

Youth in the General Population . . . . 75.6% / 24.4%

Youth in the General Population with Demographic Characteristics Similar to Youth with Disabilities . . . . 68.4% / 31.6%

Figure 1.1. Who completes school and who leaves.

estimate. In 1990–91, the average cost of education in the U.S. was $5,266 per student. On the average, the public spends 2.3 times this amount on students with disabilities. For a student with disabilities, it is estimated that an additional $6,845.80 was spent. In 1990–91, 4.8 million students with disabilities received special education services for a total additional cost of $32.86 billion. This is presented in Table 1.5.

Table 1.5
How Much Money is Spent on Special Education?

Where does the money go?		
	General Education	Special Education
Instruction	54%	62%
Support Services/Administration	35%	11%
Transportation	8%	4%
Related Services	–	10%
Public Services	3%	–
Assessment	–	13%

Where Are Students in Special Education Being Served?

During 1991–92, 4,994,169 special education students were served in the United States. It was found that 69.3 percent were served in the general classroom for almost half of the school day. Another 25.1 percent was served in a separate classroom in the regular school. We find that 4.2 percent was served in a separate school and 1.5 percent served in other places.

Who Is Providing Special Education Services?

How many special education teachers are working and how many are needed to provide services to students with disabilities? How many personnel are needed besides teachers?

During 1990–91 we had 312,682 teachers employed in special education in the United States. It was estimated that during that academic year, 1990–91 we needed an additional 29,511 teachers.

Also, during 1990–91 we had 285,822 personnel other than special education teachers employed in America. Congress estimated that we needed an additional 14,906 personnel, other than teachers, for that year.

What Happens After School

The National Longitudinal Transition study reported that postschool outcomes are better for youth who have completed secondary school, taken vocational education while in school, spent more time in general education courses, and belonged to school or community groups. The following was reported by NLTS about postschool activities for youth with disabilities:

- The NLTS reports 37% of youth with disabilities who had graduated from high school 3 to 5 years earlier had enrolled in postsecondary school as compared to 68% of the general youth population. Enrollment was lowest for youth with learning disabilities, mental retardation, and multiple impairments, while youth with sensory impairments enrolled at about the same rate as youth in general.
- Youth with disabilities were more likely to enroll in college if their parents were involved in their education in high school and expected them to go to college (NLTS).
- Youth with disabilities were about as likely as those in the general population to enroll in postsecondary vocational schools (NLTS).
- Three to five years after dropping out, 27% of dropouts with disabilities had enrolled in a program to earn a high school diploma. Eleven percent had actually earned a diploma, and 5% were still enrolled (NLTS).

Employment

- When they had been out of school 3 to 5 years, 57% of youth with disabilities were competitively employed as compared to 69% of the general population. Employment rates were highest for youth who had learning disabilities or speech impairments, and lowest for those who had multiple disabilities or orthopedic or visual impairments (NLTS).
- The rate of full-time competitive employment for youth with disabilities was 25% when they had been out of high school for 2 years. Three years later, it had risen dramatically for all disabilities to 43%. This rate is similar to the general population's full-time employment rate (46%) (NLTS).
- The wages of students who had been out of high school 3 to 5 years also increased dramatically. The percentage who earned more than $6 per hour rose to 40%. Increases were more frequent for youth who had learning disabilities, serious emotional disturbances, speech impairments, or sensory impairments. However, the median hourly wage for youth with all types of disabilities was just $5.72, less than $12,000 per year for full-time, year-round employment (NLTS).

Residential Status

- In the first 2 years out of high school, 83% of youth with disabilities lived with their parents. Three years later, 55% of this sample lived with their parents (NLTS).
- When youth with disabilities had been out of high school for 3 to 5 years, 37% were living independently—that is, alone, with a spouse or roommate, in a college dormitory, or in military housing not as a dependent. This compares to 60% of the general population. Independent living was much less common among youth with mental retardation, health impairments, or multiple disabilities (NLTS).
- About 4% of youth with disabilities lived in supervised settings, including group homes, institutions for people with disabilities, and residential schools that were not colleges. This did not change over the time of the study. Those who had multiple impairments, particularly those who were deaf/blind, were more likely to live in supervised settings (NLTS).
- Of youth with serious emotional disturbance, 10% were incarcerated or lived in drug treatment centers, shelters for the homeless, or similar settings when they had been out of high school for 3 to 5 years (NLTS).

Societal Involvement

- In 1968–87, 66% of youth in the general population who had been out of high school 3 to 5 years were registered to vote. Of students with disabilities, 51% were registered to vote (NLTS).
- By the time they had been out of high school 3 to 5 years, 15% of young men and 30% of young women with disabilities were married or living with someone of the opposite sex. These rates are similar to those in the general population (NLTS).

- The parenting rate for men was not different from that of the general population (16%), but the rate for young women with disabilities (41%) was much higher than for the general population (28%). The rate for female dropouts, 54% was even higher. One in five young single women with disabilities were mothers, and about one-third of single mothers with disabilities lived alone with their children (NLTS).

Services

- Parents reported that 30% of out-of-school youth with disabilities did not need adult services. Vocational services were needed by 60% of youth with disabilities who had been out of school for up to 5 years, and more than one-third of them were receiving these services (NLTS).
- Life skills training was reported as a need for 43% of youth with disabilities, and 30% were receiving this type of training (NLTS).

Individual Differences and Their Assessment

Terminology is important because it is the means by which we acknowledge the exceptionality itself. The terminology also gives us a springboard for learning about the individuality of the exceptional child. We all know that children of the same age vary physically. Some are tall and thin, some are short and chubby, there are red-headed ones, black-headed ones, and blond ones, and there is much variation in-between. We find this same variation in other areas such as intelligence, emotional maturity, social development, and educational attainment. These are called individual differences and they are the rule rather than the exception. It does not matter about the kind of exceptionality, children with that exceptionality will show impressive differences from one another on these characteristics. One dimension of individual differences that is extremely important is in education and in life and also our abilities and performance and how they affect the group around us. We also know that our individual genetic makeup is important as far as our abilities go. The field of genetics has advanced tremendously in the past 20 years, and we now know that more traits are influenced by our genes and chromosomes than we realized in the 1960s and 1970s. In the next few years, scientists are going to discover genes that cause many different characteristics in the human being. We know now that some characteristics clearly are linked to heredity and that intelligence, temperament, mental illness, alcoholism, criminal behavior, and vocational interest are among these characteristics.

Genetics is directly influenced by many genes and these genes which are influenced by heredity offer the makeup of the child. Instead of having just one gene, we have the influence of multiple gene interaction which seems to nudge development in one direction or another.

Individual Differences and The Classroom

Individual differences often create a serious problem for the classroom teacher. If a fourth grade class has students who are just beginning to learn the alphabet, other students who are working at an eighth grade or ninth grade level, and other students in-between those two, it makes for a real work day for the teacher. The teacher has a problem; the lesson is going to be too difficult for one child and too easy for the other, and another child is creating a problem in the classroom because he has already finished his work or he can't understand his work.

The Role of Assessment

If we examine the issue of comprehensive assessment in more depth, we will find out that there are many ways in which to assess the child. It is important, though, to realize that a child is developing on many different physical and psychological dimensions at the same time. If we are to understand a child's problems, we must keep track of individual differences in each of these dimensions.

The task of determining how an individual child is different along with how he or she is alike is a major step in identifying and educating exceptional children. We are told that assessment serves two purposes. It identifies children who are eligible for special services. Secondly, it provides information by which a teacher can plan for each individual educational plan (IEP) to meet a child's particular needs.

There are four good ways to assess the strengths and weaknesses of children. Norm-referenced tests provide a comparison of a particular child's performance against the performance of another group of children the same age such as an intelligence or achievement test. Interviews provide us information from the child, parent, teacher, or others who can provide perspective and insight into the background or historical reasons for the child's performance. Observation can provide information based on the child's spontaneous behavior in natural settings. Informal assessment is important information that we get from teacher-made tests, descriptions of significant events in the life of the child, or insights leading to effective educational planning that we get from talking to the child.

Assessment of Intelligence: Individual Tests

Most children in America are assessed for intellectual development on one of the three Wechsler intelligence scales. However, the Stanford-Binet is an intelligence test that can be used interchangeably with the Wechsler. There are four tests that are commonly accepted as the ones which we can use for placement in special education.

Stanford-Binet Intelligence Scale, 4th Edition. The fourth edition of the Stanford-Binet (SB) (Thorndike, Hagen, & Sattler, 1985) is the latest version of the scale originally developed by Alfred Binet in 1905 and revised for American children by Terman and Merrill (1916, 1937). The 1960 version of this scale combined the best items from earlier forms into one form (L–M) and provided new norms with deviation IQs. The scale was renormed in 1972, but it was not a new edition because there was not a revision of the 1960 items. The fourth edition of the Stanford-Binet maintains some continuity with the past, but also brings the SB up to date. It eliminates age scores and it is a deviation IQ test. This test can be given to persons between the ages of 2 and 23. Fifteen subtests are grouped into four areas: Verbal Reasoning, Quantitative Reasoning, Abstract/Visual Reasoning, and Short Term Memory. The authors retained as many items from the 1960 version as could fit into one of these four areas. There is an extended range of ages, therefore, not all test takers are given all subtests. A complete battery requires from 8 to 13 subtests.

The Wechsler Scales. Three different measures of intelligence have been constructed by David Wechsler. Wechsler summarized his views on the concept of intelligence by stating that intelligence is a global thing. The original Wechsler scale, the Wechsler-Bellview Intelligence Scale (1939), was designed to assist the intelligence of adults and was revised in 1955 and called the Wechsler Adult Intelligence Scale (WAIS). Its present form in called the Wechsler Adult Intelligence Scale—Revised (WAIS–R). In 1949, Wechsler developed the Wechsler Intelligence Scale for Children (WISC). This scale was revised and restandardized in 1974 and again in 1991. Its present form was developed by personnel at the Psychological Corporation and is called the Wechsler Intelligence Scale for Children—III (WISC–III). In 1967, Wechsler developed a downward extension of the WISC, the Wechsler Preschool and Primary Scale of Intelligence (WPPSI). The WPPSI was revised and restandardized in 1989 and is now called the WPPSI–R. Although the three scales are similar in form and content, they are distinct scales designed for use with persons at different age levels. The WAIS–R is designed to be used with individuals over the age of 16; the WISC–III is designed to assess the intelligence of children and youth between the ages 6–16; the WPPSI–R is designed to be used with children ages 3–7¼. All three scales are point scales, all three include both a verbal and a performance section, and all three have a full scale IQ. The three Wechsler tests are by far the most utilized intelligence tests in America.

ACADEMIC PERFORMANCE

There are two well-accepted approaches to tracking interindividual differences in academic performance and they are the standard norm-referenced achievement test and the diagnostic achievement test. The standard (norm-referenced) achievement test measures the student's level of achievement and compares that with students of a similar age or grade throughout the nation. These tests tell us whether the student is achieving at expected levels or if he is achieving below expected levels, but they do not tell us why the student is not performing as well as he or she should be. **Diagnostic achievement tests** help determine the process the student is using to solve a problem or decode a reading passage so that we can understand why a particular student is not mastering some aspect of the school curriculum. For example, we can tell why he or she is not performing at the level of other students.

For example, we can use an informal reading inventory and tell what kinds of mistakes that a student is making in his reading and also why he is not solving a certain problem. An analysis of the errors a student makes will reveal a student's problems.

LANGUAGE DEVELOPMENT

Language is one of the most complex of human functions and is quite vulnerable to problems affecting the development of children. Because using language effectively is such a key to academic success, it is a dimension that we should carefully analyze, particularly when a student is not performing well. We have receptive language (listening) and expressive language (speaking) and they often need a separate assessment. The Test of Adolescent Language-II (Hammill, Brown, Larsen, & Weiderholt, 1987) is used to examine the dimensions of listening/vocabulary, listening/grammar, speaking/vocabulary, speaking/grammar, reading/vocabulary, reading/grammar, writing/vocabulary, and writing/

grammar. This is a comprehensive measure which allows the special educator to find areas of relative strength and weakness in a child's linguistic processes and this test will allow the educator to develop some specific plans for an individualized program of instruction after he has found the student's weaknesses.

PSYCHOSOCIAL DEVELOPMENT

A very important area of interindividual differences is the child's ability to respond to his social environment or how well the child is able to adapt. Does a particular child show aggressive tendencies when frustrated? Is this child able to work cooperatively with others? How does the child react when things don't go right? When the child is in certain social interactions, how will he act toward his teachers and peers?

Social adaptation also greatly influences how a handicapped child responds to remediation. Many handicapped children who fail to respond to special programs have behavioral and social problems. These problems lead to academic problems. It is difficult to remediate a reading disability if a child has a severe emotional problem or becomes aggressive when frustrated. For this reason, special educators often focus on behavioral and social problems at the same time that they tackle the academic difficulties of a specific child.

When we assess psychosocial development, we often rely on observation by ourselves and others—parents, teachers, and caregivers. We get information from these people about how the child behaves in different settings. There are several rating scales that can be used to help us in our judgments about children.

Another strategy is to have the teacher systematically observe the child at school. In this way we can catalog the child's typical patterns of behavior. When children are able to speak or to articulate, we can ask them about their feelings about themselves and their home life. These self-reports can be quite revealing. They might show that a mentally retarded child or a child with specific learning disabilities has a very low self-concept that is keeping him from functioning up to his capabilities.

Most of our information about the adaptive behavior of the mildly handicapped child or the exceptional child comes from direct observation or from interviews with family members and teachers, but we also have adaptive behavior scales such as the AAMD Adaptive Behavior Scale, the Vineland Social Maturity Scale, or the Burk's Behavior Rating Scales. These scales are used to measure the social adaptability of children and to determine if they are emotionally disturbed, aggressive, passive, or if they have other traits which interfere with learning.

The study of special education is the study of differences. The exceptional child is different in some way from the "average" child or youth. This type of child may have problems or special talents in thinking, seeing, hearing, speaking, socializing, or moving. Generally, such a child has a combination of special abilities or disabilities. Today, almost 5 million handicapped children have been identified in the public schools throughout America and this does not include children in the gifted and talented programs. This book is about the mildly handicapped though, and the gifted and talented child will not be discussed. There are many misconceptions about special education which need to be dispelled (see Table 1.6).

PREVALENCE OF DISABLED CHILDREN

According to a profile published in *Exceptional Children* (1994) there were 4,994,169 students served in special education in the United States during the school year 1991–92 (see Figure 1.2).

Before considering the difficulties of determining the prevalence of handicapping conditions, we need to clarify the statistical terminology used in most reports on the numbers of handicapped children.

The terms **incidence** and **prevalence** are often used interchangeably in speaking of the number of exceptional children. Technically, **incidence** refers to the number of new cases of children with exceptionality in a given period of time (usually a year). **Prevalence** applies to the total number of existing cases (new and old) in the population at a given point in time. For instance, we might find that the **incidence** of blindness among children in New York City was 200 for 1994, meaning that in 1994 there were 200 new cases of blindness in children. We might find too that the **prevalence** of blindness in the child population of New York City in 1994 was 3,000, meaning that in 1994 there were 3,000 blind children in New York City. **Prevalence** is also used to refer to the percent of proportion of the population that falls into a given category. Thus we might state the prevalence of blindness in New York City in 1994 was 0.03 percent, indicating that 3 of every 10,000 children in New York City were blind in 1994. Obviously, establishing accurate figures depends on obtaining accurate counts of the number of handicapped and nonhandicapped children in the population in question.

Table 1.6
Misconceptions About Special Education

Myth	Fact
Special education originated in America.	The origins of special education are found in the work of nineteenth-century European physicians.
Public schools may choose not to provide education for some children.	Federal legislation specifies that in order to receive federal funds, every school system must provide a free, appropriate education for every child regardless of any handicapping condition.
By law, the handicapped child must be placed in the least restrictive environment (LRE). The LRE is always the regular classroom.	Law does require that the handicapped child be placed in the LRE. However, LRE is not always the regular classroom. What LRE does mean is that the handicapped child shall be segregated as little as possible from home, family, community, and the regular class setting. In many, but certainly not all, instances this will mean placement in the regular classroom.
It is a relatively easy matter to determine the prevalence of exceptional children.	A host of variables--vague and changing definitions, overlapping diagnoses, sampling errors, school-defined nature of exceptionality, and the deliberate avoidance by some of having their children labeled exceptional--make it exceedingly difficult to arrive at accurate prevalence figures.
The causes of most disabilities are known, but little is known about how to help children overcome or compensate for their disabilities.	In most cases, the causes of children's disabilities are not known, although progress is being made in pinpointing why many disabilities occur. More is known about the treatment of most disabilities than about their causes.

THE AMERICANS WITH DISABILITIES ACT OF 1990

As stated earlier in this chapter, President George Bush, on July 26, 1990, signed into law the most sweeping civil rights legislation in the United States since the **Civil Rights Act of 1964:** the **Americans with Disabilities Act (ADA)** (Public Law 101-336). The purpose of ADA was to provide a national mandate to end discrimination against individuals with disabilities in private-sector employment, all public services,

Who is being served in special education?

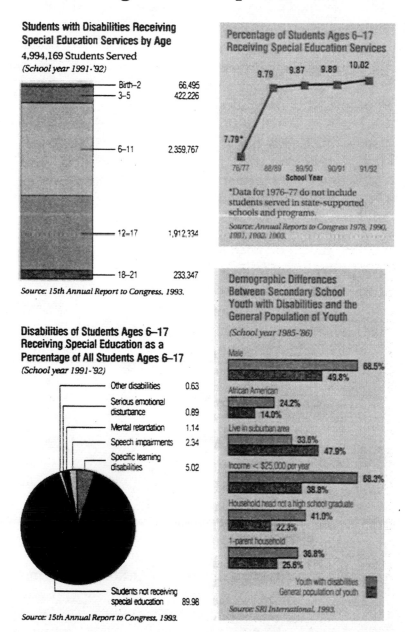

Students with Disabilities Receiving Special Education Services by Age
4,994,169 Students Served
(School year 1991-'92)

Age	Students
Birth–2	66,495
3–5	422,226
6–11	2,359,767
12–17	1,912,334
18–21	233,347

Source: 15th Annual Report to Congress, 1993.

Percentage of Students Ages 6–17 Receiving Special Education Services

9.79   9.87   9.89   10.02

7.79*

76/77   88/89   89/90   90/91   91/92
School Year

*Data for 1976–77 do not include students served in state-supported schools and programs.

Source: Annual Reports to Congress 1978, 1990, 1991, 1992, 1993.

Disabilities of Students Ages 6–17 Receiving Special Education as a Percentage of All Students Ages 6–17
(School year 1991-'92)

Other disabilities	0.63
Serious emotional disturbance	0.89
Mental retardation	1.14
Speech impairments	2.34
Specific learning disabilities	5.02
Students not receiving special education	89.98

Source: 15th Annual Report to Congress, 1993.

Demographic Differences Between Secondary School Youth with Disabilities and the General Population of Youth
(School year 1985-'86)

	Youth with disabilities	General population of youth
Male	68.5%	49.8%
African American	24.2%	14.0%
Live in suburban area	33.5%	47.9%
Income < $25,000 per year	68.3%	38.8%
Household head not a high school graduate	41.0%	22.3%
1-parent household	36.8%	25.8%

Source: SRI International, 1993.

Figure 1.2. Statistical profile of special education in the United States, 1994.

and public accommodations, transportation, and telecommunications. The legislation defined a person with a disability as (1) having a physical or mental impairment that substantially limits him or her in some major life activity and (2) having experienced discrimination resulting from this physical or mental impairment. ADA charged the federal government with the task of ensuring that these provisions be enforced on behalf of all people with disabilities (West, 1991).

Hardman, Drew, et al. tell us that such legislation, coming almost 30 years after the Civil Rights Act of 1964, was truly needed for several reasons. First, it was clear that people with disabilities were being discriminated against in employment, access to public and private accommodations (e.g., hotels, theaters, restaurants, grocery stores), and services offered through state and local governments. Second, the historic Civil Rights Act of 1964 did not even mention people with disabilities. Therefore, these individuals had no federal protection against discrimination except through some limited provisions in **Section 504 of the Vocational Rehabilitation Act of 1973** (Public Law 93-112). Senator Tom Harkin, a leading proponent of ADA in the U.S. Senate, suggested that:

> Discrimination is sometimes the result of prejudice; sometimes it is the result of patronizing attitudes; and still other times it is the result of thoughtlessness or indifference. Whatever its origin, the results are the same: segregation, exclusion, or denial of equal, effective and meaningful opportunities to participate in programs and opportunities. (Harkin, 1990, p. 1)

THE INDIVIDUAL WITH DISABILITIES EDUCATION ACT OF 1990

In 1990, Congress amended the Education of the Handicapped Act and introduced some significant changes to its original mandate, including P.L. 94-142 (Part B of EHA). The most important of these changes obviously was renaming the law the Individual with Disabilities Education Act (IDEA) (P.L. 101-476). IDEA expanded the definition of special education to include instruction in all settings. This includes the work place as well as training centers. As was true with P.L. 94-142, IDEA also stipulated that students with disabilities had to receive any related services that would ensure that they benefitted from their educational experience.

Under IDEA, the following conditions merit special services: children with mental retardation, specific learning disabilities, serious emotional disturbances, speech and language impairment, visual impairment, including blindness, hearing impairment, othopedic impairment, other health impairments, autism, and traumatic brain injury. Autism and traumatic brain injury were added to the list. According to Hardman, Drew et al. (1993), IDEA provided for:

1. **nondiscriminatory and multidisciplinary assessment** of educational needs
2. Parental involvement in developing each child's educational program
3. Education in the **least restrictive environment (LRE)**
4. An **individualized education program (IEP)**

Nondiscriminatory and multidisciplinary assessment. IDEA incorporated several provisions related to the use of nondiscriminatory testing procedures in labeling and placement of students for special education services. Those provisions include:

1. The testing of students in their native or primary language, whenever possible
2. The use of evaluation procedures selected and administered to prevent cultural or racial discrimination
3. The use of assessment tools validated for the purpose for which they are being used
4. Assessment by a **multidisciplinary team** utilizing several pieces of information to formulate a placement decision

Students with disabilities were too often placed in special education programs on the basis of inadequate or invalid assessment information. One result of such oversights was a disproportionate number of ethnic minority children and children from low-socioeconomic-level backgrounds being placed in special education programs.

Parent involvement in the educational process. IDEA described the role of parents in the education of their children. Parents were granted rights to:

1. Consent in writing before the child is initially evaluated
2. Consent in writing before the child is initially placed in a special education program
3. Request an independent education evaluation if they feel the school's evaluation is inappropriate
4. Request an evaluation at public expense if a due-process hearing finds that the public agency's evaluation was inappropriate
5. Participate on the committee that considers the evaluation, placement, and programming of the child
6. Inspect and review educational records and challenge information believed to be inaccurate, misleading, or in violation of the privacy or other rights of the child
7. Request a copy of information from the child's educational record
8. Request a hearing concerning the school's proposal or refusal to initiate or change the identification, evaluation, or placement of the child or the provision of a free, appropriate public education (p. 25).

Table 1.7 presents the Highlights of Federal Education Policy for Children with Disabilities up through 1991.

Table 1.7
Highlights of Federal Education Policy for Children with Disabilities

Title	Purpose
PL 85-926 (1958)	Provided grants for teaching children with handicaps; related to education of children who are mentally retarded
PL 88-164, Title III (1963)	Authorized funds for teacher training and for reserarch and demonstration projects in the education of persons with handicaps
PL 89-10 (1965)	Elementary and Secondary Education Act, Title III authorized assistance to children with handicaps in state-operated and state-supported private day and residential schools
PL 89-13	Amendments to PL 89-10; provided grants to state educational agencies for the education of children with handicaps in state-supported institutions
PL 90-170 (1967)	Amendments to PL 88-164; provided funds for personnel training to care for individuals who are mentally retarded; included individuals with neurological conditions related to mental retardation
PL 90-247 (1968)	Amendments to PL 89-10; provided regional resource centers for the improvement of education of children with handicaps
PL 90-538 (1968)	Handicapped Children's Early Education Assistance Act; provided grants for the development and implementation of experimental programs in early education for children with handicaps, from birth to age 6
PL 91-230 (1969)	Amendments to PL 89-10; Title VI consolidated into one act--Education of the Handicapped--the previous enactments related to children with handicaps
PL 92-424 (1972)	Economic Opportunity Amendments; required that not less than 10 percent of Head Start enrollment opportunities be available to children with handicaps
PL 93-380 (1974)	Amended and expanded Education of the Handicapped Act (PL 910-230) in response to right-to-education mandates; required stated to establish goal for providing full educational opportunity for all children with handicaps, birth to age 21
PL 94-142 (1975)	Education for All Handicapped Children Act; required states to provide by September 1, 1978, a free appropriate education for all children with handicaps betweeen the ages of 3 and 18
PL 98-199 (1984)	Amended the Handicapped Children's Early Education Assistance Act (PL 90-538); provided funds for planning statewide comprehensive services for children with handicaps through age 5
PL 99-457, Part H (1986)	Amended the Education of the Handicapped Act; mandated comprehensive multidisciplinary services for infants and toddlers (birth through age 2) and their families
PL 101-476 (1990)	Individuals with Disabilities Education Act (IDEA); required schools to provide transition services to all students with disabilities
PL 101-336 (1991)	Americans with Disabilities Act; Reaffirms the rights of disabled individuals to equal access to facilities and opportunities

A MANDATE FOR PRESCHOOL CHILDREN WITH DISABILITIES

In 1986, Congress amended the Education of the Handicapped Act (now IDEA) to include provisions for preschool age children with disabilities. This important legislation, P.L. 99-457, established a new mandate to provide a free and appropriate education for all children with disabilities ages three through five. P.L. 99-457, Part H of 1986 amended the Education of the Handicapped Act and mandated comprehensive multidisciplinary services for infants and toddlers birth through age two. At the present time all children having disabilities from birth through 21 are covered under federal legislation.

THE MILDLY HANDICAPPED CHILD IN THE SCHOOL

Schools to a great degree, are a mirror of our society as a whole. Most of the values taught at school reflect the values of the dominant sectors of society. Many of the problems encountered in the school, such as lack of motivation, drug use, and violence, are a part of the larger societal fabric.

The school environment is where the many forces that act on exceptional children interact and influence each other. Our laws regulate who is taught and how. The courts interpret those laws and apply them to specific circumstances and families either support or do not support the child's efforts. The families also provide goals, values, and expectations that generally reflect the family's cultural background. The school is particularly important for mildly handicapped children who may need very special kinds of help to become productive adults.

SPECIAL EDUCATION ADAPTATION

The nature of special education is to provide mildly handicapped children with services that are not available to them in the regular classrooms. Special education programs are different from regular programs because they try to take into account the child's interindividual and intraindividual differences. It is important to realize that special education does not exist because regular education has failed. Special education and regular education should go hand in hand to enhance the child's chances of success. Classroom teachers and typical education programs simply cannot respond fully to the special needs of exceptional children without a substantial change in the structure, program, and staffing of a classroom.

The concept of least restrictive environment means the teacher's attempt to educate a child in the environmental setting that is best suited to the child's individual learning motif. In the resource room, the teacher is there to work with a small group of children at any time during the school day. The child will be evaluated by a multidisciplinary team and his or her educational needs will be outlined to the special education teacher and the regular classroom teacher. The child may spend only 75 minutes per day with the special education resource teacher working on math and reading and spend the rest of the day in the regular classroom. A child can spend up to three hours per day in the resource room. Therefore, that child would spend three hours per day in the regular classroom.

Figure 1.3 indicates the percentage of children who spend time in a resource room, regular class, separate class, separate facility, home or hospital, and residential setting. The recent emphasis on the regular classroom education and on mainstreaming often leaves the impression that practically all exceptional children are now back in the regular classroom. This is far from the case. Figure 1.3 summarizes where students with handicapping conditions are served. One out of every four disabled students is being educated in a totally separate class, more than 5 percent are being educated in a separate facility, such as a separate school, and a very small number of exceptional children are placed in residential or hospital settings. From Figure 1.3 it is clear that the most popular of the learning environment adaptations is the resource room or pull-out program, followed by a regular class placement.

Special Education Classrooms in Schools. It is the view of many professionals and parents that neither the consulting teacher model nor the resource room model is appropriate to meet certain students' needs. These students often require more intensive and specialized educational services provided in either a self-contained special education classroom or a special school for students with disabilities.

The Self-Contained Special Education Classroom. The self-contained special education classroom employs the expertise of a qualified special education teacher to work with a group of students who are disabled for most of the school day. This one teacher could work with the students all of the school day. This teacher may still create opportunities for students with disabilities to interact with nondisabled peers whenever appropriate, for instance, through academically and nonacademically oriented classes, lunch, playground activities, school events, peer-tutor programs, and so forth.

The Special School. Students with disabilities may also be placed in special schools. There are proponents of this arrangement who have argued that special schools provide services for large numbers of disabled students and, therefore, provide greater homogeneity in grouping and programming. For example, many people argue for a special school

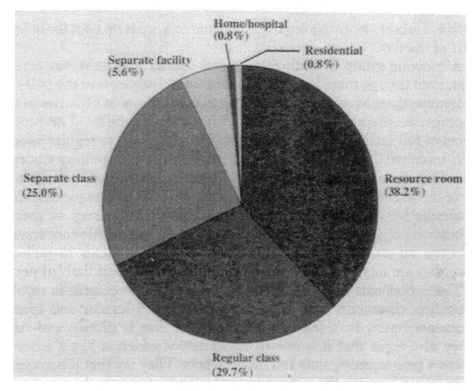

Figure 1.3. Percentage of students with handicaps ages 3–21.

where blind and partially sighted students should go, and also, a facility where the deaf and hearing impaired should go. Proponents have also argued that special schools provide for the centralization of supplies, equipment, and special facilities.

The Resource Room. The resource room is one of the pull-out programs. A child spends part of each day in the regular classroom and goes to the resource room teacher for instruction in special subjects, such as reading, math, spelling, or even English. A student can spend up to three hours per day in the resource room, but many students only spend 30 minutes to an hour with the resource room teacher working on special problems.

FULL INCLUSION VS. PULL-OUT PROGRAMS

The philosophy behind resource rooms and self-contained special education classrooms have been the predominant instructional approach for students with disabilities over the past twenty years. This approach is commonly referred to as pull-out programs or removing the student with a disability from the regular classroom to a separate class for at least part of the day.

A growing group of both regular and special educators has agreed that, even though there have been some accomplishments in the pull-out programs, there have also been several negative effects or obstacles to the appropriate education of each child who has a disability. The proponents of full inclusion, which is sometimes referred to as regular education initiative, have argued that the current system of pulling students out of regular education simply does not work. They argue that it fails to serve the individualized needs of each student. They also argue that such programs result in a fragmented approach to the delivery of special education programs. These people also say that there is little cooperation between regular and special education teachers. Students in pull-out programs are stigmatized when segregated from their nondisabled peers.

The proponents of full inclusion also argue that placement in regular education classrooms with a partnership between regular and special educators results in a learning environment that is diverse and rich. They also argue that it is not an environment which is just a series of discreet programming slots and funding pots. They say that it becomes a partnership between the regular and special education teachers and each student's instructional program is implemented by two different teachers and also, the child is really in the least restrictive environment. Additionally, special educators are more effective in a partnership, proponents say, because they can bring their knowledge and resources to assist regular educators to develop strategies that are directly oriented to the students' needs in a natural setting which is the regular classroom.

Of course, there are opponents to full inclusion. They have argued that regular education has little expertise in assisting students with learning problems and that the regular class teacher is already overburdened with large class sizes and inadequate support services. Special educators have been specifically trained to develop instructional strategies and use teaching techniques in a resource room or in a self-contained classroom, they also argue. They say that more specialized academic and social instruction can be provided in a pull-out setting and thus the special education student will get a better education. Specialized pull-out settings also allow for concentration of both human and material resources.

There is a question which is appropriate to both supporters and detractors of shared responsibility in the special education pull-out vs.

full inclusion in regular classrooms for students with disabilities. Jenkins et al. (1990) have formulated several questions that need to be addressed by schools in assessing their readiness if they are intending to have full inclusion:

1. To what extent do classroom teachers accept responsibilities for
   a. educating all students assigned to them,
   b. making and monitoring major instructional decisions for all students in their class,
   c. providing instruction that follows a normal developmental curriculum in the basic skills area that is designed to bring students to a level of adult competence,
   d. managing instruction for diverse populations, and
   e. seeking, using, and coordinating assistance for students who require more intense service than those provided to their peers?

2. To what extent do principals have sufficient knowledge about instruction and learning to distribute resources across so that students with special needs can be accommodated and served effectively?

3. To what extent are "specialists" ... able to collaborate and communicate with classroom teachers and relinquish to them final authority regarding instructional decision making?

4. To what extent are multidisciplinary teams prepared to require hard evidence that students have received high-quality direct instruction from classroom teachers and support staff?

5. Are multidisciplinary teams prepared to decide that students will not develop competency in basic skills during their school career, and recommend that the students be segregated from their regular classroom peers? (pp. 481–482, 189)

AN INSTRUCTIONAL DECISION-MAKING MODEL

Learning is a continual process of adaptation for students who have disabilities and who attempt to cope with the demands of school. These students learn to adapt to a limited time restraint placed on them by our educational system. They do not learn as quickly or as effectively as other children do and are constantly fighting a battle against failure. These children must somehow learn to deal with a system that is often rigid and one which allows little room for learning or behavior differences. Our students with mild disabilities must also be able to adapt to a teaching process that may be oriented toward the majority of students within a regular classroom and not based on individualized assessment of needs or personalized instruction.

In spite of many obstacles, students with disabilities can learn to survive in the educational environment as well as develop socially and also develop academic skills which can orient them toward striving for success rather than fighting against failure. Success for these children can be achieved only if a professional team remains flexible, adapting to meet the needs of these students.

An educational team plays an important role in creating the adaptive fit between the school environment and the needs of our special students. This team must make a critical decision concerning educational goals and objectives. This team must also make decisions about the appropriate curricula and the least restrictive environment alternatives. The magnitude of the decisions is illustrated in Figure 1.4 which shows a three-dimensional model for instructional decision making. As you can see, the first dimension of this model represents the curricular approaches that may be used to teach students who have disabilities. The second dimension focuses on the processes involved in teaching, including assessment, and also planning, implementation and the evaluation of the program. The third dimension, as one can see, is temporal. Since only so much instructional time is available from early childhood through the secondary period, it is difficult to make decisions about what must be taught and when an educational experience is appropriate for a particular child.

These three curricular approaches may be used in teaching students. The first approach or primary approach, termed the *learning of basic skills,* stresses that the student must learn a specific set of sequenced skills, each of which is a stepping stone for the next. This process is often referred to as the developmental approach and can be analyzed by looking at the way we teach reading.

The reading process is a blend of many special skills which must work in harmony. If one skill or several skills are missing, the entire process breaks down. If the process breaks down, a child may very well be unable to read or comprehend. The teaching of basic reading can be divided into three phases: (1) reading readiness, left to right sequential, visual and auditory discrimination skills, etc; (2) the development of word recognition or decoding skills; and (3) the development of reading comprehension. The basic skills approach, whether in reading or any other content area, lays the groundwork for the further development so that a child may go on to a higher level of functioning.

We realize that not all children learn the basic skills within the time frame dictated by the schools. We know that many alternatives are available to educators and special educators to assist students who do not

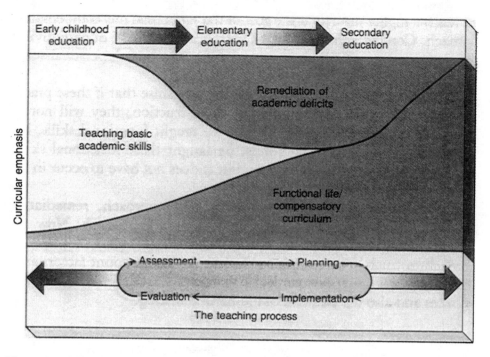

Figure 1.4. An instructional decision-making model. From *Human Exceptionality: Society, School, and the Family* (Fifth Edition) by M.L. Hardman, C.J. Drew, M.W. Egan, and B. Wolf, 1996, Allyn and Bacon. Copyright 1996 by Allyn and Bacon. Reprinted by permission.

learn in the traditional way. One alternative is to remediate deficiencies in the student's repertoire of basic skills. This is called the remediation approach and certain deficiencies are identified by determining what skills the student has and the skills that the student does not have. We must then locate appropriate materials and instructional approaches to achieve mastery of those skills. This approach focuses on helping the learner to adapt to the content and method of instruction that is provided for a majority of students in our typical learning classroom. Skilled efficiencies may be the result of either poor teaching or a lack of ability on the part of the student. It is doubtful that the learner's behavior can be changed by simply repeating that which resulted in failure. Teaching must be more systematic and precise if these deficits are to be remediated.

Another alternative for special educators is to teach skills using a functional/compensatory life approach. Following this approach, students are taught only those skills that will facilitate their accommodation to a natural setting whether it is the classroom, family, or neighborhood. The skills necessary for a person to control and modify his environment and reach a higher priority is the goal of the functional life/compensatory approach. Content areas are taught within a framework of daily living, self-care, consumer financing, community travel, and personal-social development.

This functional approach is based on the premise that if these practical skills are not taught through formal instruction, they will not be learned. Most students do not need to be taught functional skills, but our special education students must be taught these functional skills. Instruction may occur in these areas, but it does not have to occur in the same sequence as in the basic skills approach.

The author has discussed the basic-skills approach, remediation approach, and the functional life/compensatory approach. Now the educational team is confronted with the difficult decision about which approach to teach. These decisions must take into account factors such as the student's age, previous learning history, and the availability of resources and also the demand of the natural setting.

REFERENCES

Hammill, D., Brown, V., Larsen, S., & Weiderholt, L. (1987). *Test of Adolescent Language—2.* Austin, TX: Pro-ed.

Hardman, M., Drew, C., Egan, W., & Wolf, B. (1993). *Human exceptionality.* Boston: Allyn & Bacon.

Haselkorn, D., & Calkins, A. (1993). *Careers in teaching handbook.* Belmont, MA: Recruiting New Teachers, Inc.

Henderson, C. (1992). *College freshmen with disabilities: A statistical profile.* Washington, DC: American Council of Education, HEATH Resource Center. (ERIC No. ED354792).

Kirk, S., Gallagher, J., & Anastasiow, N. (1993). *Educating exceptional children.* Boston: Houghton Mifflin.

Moore, M. (1988, December). *Patterns in special education service delivery and cost.* Washington, DC: Decision Resources Corporation. (ERIC No. ED303027).

National Longitudinal Transition Study of Special Education Students (NLTS). (1994, January). Supplement to *Teaching Exceptional Children,* Vol. 26, No. 3.

Office of Civil Rights, U.S. Department of Education. (1992, February). *National and state summaries of data from the 1990 elementary and secondary school civil rights survey* (unpublished data available from the U.S. Office for Civil Rights.)

SRI International. (1993, December 9). *Action Seminar: The transition experiences of young people with disabilities Implications for policy and programs. Briefing materials.* Menlo Park, CA: SRI International.

Thorndike, R. L., Hagen, E., & Sattler, J. (1985). *Stanford-Binet Intelligence Scale.* Chicago: The Riverside Publishing Co.

U.S. Department of Education, Office of Special Education Programs. (1978–1993).

First-fifteenth annual reports to Congress on the implementation of the Individuals with Disabilities Education Act. Washington, DC: Author.

U.S. Department of Education, National Center for Education Statistics, Schools and Staffing Survey. (1987–88). (Unpublished data.)

Wagner, M. (1991, September). *Drop outs with disabilities: What do we know? What can we do?* Menlo Park, CA: SRI International.

Wagner, M., D'Amico, R., Marder, C., Newman, L., & Blackorby, J. (1992, December). *What happens next? Trends in postschool outcomes of youth with disabilities.* Menlo Park, CA: SRI International.

Wechsler, D. (1967). *Manual for the Wechsler Preschool and Primary Scale of Intelligence.* Cleveland, OH: The Psychological Corp.

Wechsler, D. (1974). *Manual for the Wechsler Intelligence Scale for Children—Revised.* Cleveland, OH: The Psychological Corp.

Wechsler, D. (1981). *Manual for the Wechsler Adult Intelligence Scale—Revised.* New York: The Psychological Corp.

Wechsler, D. (1991). *Wechsler Intelligence Scale for Children-III.* San Antonio, TX: Psychological Corp.

West, J. (1991). Implementing the act: Where do we begin? In J. West (Ed.), *The Americans with Disabilities Act: From policy to practice* (pp. xi–xxxi). New York: Millbank Memorial Fund.

Chapter 2

PHYSICAL DISABILITIES
AND HEALTH IMPAIRMENTS

IDEA uses the term "other health impairments" to distinguish these conditions from the physical disabilities involving muscles, joints, and bones. Using the three major criteria, limited strength, vitality, or alertness which affect a student's educational needs, IDEA defines other health impairments (OHI) as follows:

> Having limited strength, vitality, or alertness due to chronic or acute health problems such as heart condition, tuberculosis, rheumatic fever, nephritis, asthma, sickle cell anemia, hemophilia, seizure disorder, lead poisoning, leukemia, or diabetes that adversely affect a child's educational performance.

Please notice that IDEA emphasizes that the condition can be chronic or acute. A chronic condition develops slowly and the symptoms are long lasting. An acute condition develops quickly and the symptoms are intense, but it lasts for a relatively short period of time. Some conditions, such as asthma, are chronic but the episodes are acute and subside suddenly.

DEFINING PHYSICAL DISABILITIES

There is a great deal of confusion about the definition of physical disabilities. IDEA refers to physical disabilities as orthopedic impairments.

> "Orthopedic impairment" means a severe orthopedic impairment that adversely affects a child's educational performance. The term includes impairments caused by congenital anomaly (e.g., clubfoot, absence of some member, etc.), impairments caused by disease (e.g., poliomyelitis, bone tuberculosis, etc.), and impairments from other causes (e.g., cerebral palsy, amputations, and fractures or burns that cause contractures).

HUMAN IMMUNODEFICIENCY VIRUS

Many students not only have to deal with their medical problems, but they also must do it under a veil of secrecy. Many parents tell their HIV children not to talk to anyone about why they are sick.

What is HIV? HIV is a condition that gradually infects and eventually destroys the very important cells in the body's immune system which protects us from disease. These children must have T4 cell counts often because T4 immune cells are a major target of HIV. When HIV destroys the T4 cells and other immune cells the body becomes increasingly unable to fight infection.

Pregnant women can transmit the HIV to their unborn children. There is no known cure for the disease, which is fatal. It is estimated that between 1 and 1.5 million people in the United States are infected with the HIV and projections of the number of people who may get the disease and die are staggering.

Only a small number of young children diagnosed with AIDS have survived to school-age; however, with the continuing development of drug treatments to slow the progression of the disease, the likelihood is great that children with AIDS will be in the classroom. Children with HIV infection and AIDS are afforded legal protection and the right to a public education. Section 504 of the Rehabilitation Act of 1973 states,

> No otherwise qualified individual with handicaps . . . shall solely by reason of his handicap be excluded from the participation in, be denied the benefits of, or be subjected to discrimination under any program or activity receiving Federal financial assistance.

In 1990, a memorandum from the Office of Civil Rights stated that a child with AIDS "generally will be considered 'handicapped' under Section 504 due to the substantial limitation on a major life activity caused by either physical impairment or the reaction of others to the perceived disease."

On the basis of the knowledge we presently have concerning AIDS, Byers (1989) suggests the following implications and recommendations:

1. We certainly must continue with an AIDS curriculum in grades K–12 in an effort to prevent the disease from further infiltrating the pre-adolescent and adolescent populations.
2. Children harboring the virus cannot legally be excluded from schools unless they are deemed a direct health risk for other children (e.g., exhibit biting behavior, open sores). Consequently, chronic illness specialists, school psychologists, counselors, and teachers will need to make AIDS a priority issue, and be active in facilitating school/peer acceptance and the social adjustment of a child with AIDS.
3. Teachers, counselors, and other specialists will also need to be prepared to provide family therapy and broad-based support groups for parents and/or children within the school setting.

4. Pediatric AIDS patients present a particular challenge for special education professionals, due to the erratic course of neurological deterioration. The child may be stable for a number of months and then deteriorate rapidly over a period of weeks (Epstein et al., 1988), and thus require regular monitoring of his or her educational needs.

5. Specific educational treatments for children infected with HIV await further research, and this appears to be the ultimate challenge for special educators (p. 13).

BURNS

Burns are a leading kind of injury in childhood. Burns are sometimes caused by child abuse, but generally come about because of household accidents. We know that the skin is the largest organ in the human body and one of the most important. Serious burns often cause complications in other organs, infections, long-term physical limitations, and psychological problems.

Children with serious burn injuries usually experience pain, scarring, limitations of motion, lengthy hospitalizations, and repeated surgery (Heward, 1995). Some children with facial burns must wear sterile elastic masks to protect and soften the skin. Yurt and Pruitt (1983) tell us that:

> The disfigurement caused by severe burns can affect a child's behavior and self-image, especially if teachers and peers react negatively. When a child is returning to class after prolonged absence resulting from an extensive burn injury, it may be advisable for the teacher, parents, or other involved person (e.g., a social worker, physical therapist) to explain to classmates the nature of the child's injury and appearance.

ASTHMA

Asthma is a condition that affects the lungs and causes breathing difficulties. Some people with asthma have only occasional symptoms while others experience breathing difficulties almost daily. Symptoms may be mild or they may be life-threatening.

What Is Asthma?

Asthma, which is the most common lung disease among children, begins in about half the childhood cases before age three. About twice as many boys have asthma as girls, and boys are more likely to have severe asthma. The general tendency is for asthma symptoms in boys to decrease with age, but for girls to experience more problems as they go into adolescence.

Asthma has three primary features (National Heart, Lung, and Blood Institute, 1992):

- Airway linings are swollen.
- Airways narrow and breathing becomes difficult. This narrowing may reverse (but not completely in some people) by itself or with treatment.
- Airways are hypersensitive or are supersensitive. They react to a variety of stimuli, or triggers, including physical changes (cold air or exercise), allergens (cat dander, dust mites, and molds), and irritants (smoke, strong odors, and sprays). Coughing, wheezing, or difficult breathing—also known as asthma attacks or episodes—may occur.

The National Education Program (1991) classifies individuals as having mild, moderate, or severe asthma.

Paul and Fatoglia (1988) say that:

Although most individuals you encounter with asthma will probably only have mild or moderate symptoms, asthma can cause a medical emergency and, in rare cases (about five thousand per year), lead to death. If you have a student who has the following symptoms, you should seek emergency treatment immediately.

- Over a period of three to four days, asthma symptoms cannot be controlled with usual medications.
- The individual experiences more asthma symptoms than usual over a period of several hours.
- To feel relief, the person needs to take medication more often than prescribed.
- Mucous secretions cannot be cleared by coughing.

Turnbull, Turnbull, Shank and Leal (1995) describe the following three rules when dealing with students with asthma:

1. *Asthma in the Classroom.* When you have a student with asthma in your class, it is important to know some basic preventions and treatments. For students with asthma, these include taking medications, monitoring lung functioning, managing stress and exercise, and controlling triggers.
2. *Taking Medications.* Physicians commonly prescribe anti-inflammatory drugs and bronchial dilators, such as Orlando's capsule in his book bag. Students with mild asthma only need medication when an asthma episode occurs. For others whose asthma interferes with routine activities, sleep, or exercise, daily medications are useful.
3. *Monitoring Lung Functioning.* Your student might also monitor lung functioning through the use of a peak flow meter. To operate the device, a person with asthma simply exhales as hard as possible into the mouthpiece. The higher the reading, the better the lungs are working. Lower readings indicate that the airways are obstructed (p. 422).

SPINA BIFIDA

For every 2,000 infants born in the United States, one will have a congenital defect in the vertebrae that enclose the spinal cord. As a result of this defect, a portion of the spinal cord and the nerves that normally control muscles and feeding in the lower part of the body fail to develop normally. There are three types of spina bifida and the mildest form is spina bifida occulta in which only a few vertebrae are malformed, usually in the lower spine. This type of defect sometimes is not even visible externally. If the flexible casings (meninges) that surround the spinal cord bulge through an opening in the infant's back when he is born, the condition is called meningocele. As a general rule, these two forms do not usually cause any loss of human function. However, in the most common form of spina bifida, which is myelomeningocele, the spinal lining, spinal cord, and nerve roots all protrude. The protruding spinal cord and nerves generally are tucked back into the spinal column shortly after birth. This third type is the most serious condition carrying a high risk of paralysis, infection, mental retardation, paraplegia, and hydrocephalus.

About 80 to 90 percent of children born with spina bifida develop hydrocephalus which is an accumulation of cerebrospinal fluid in tissues surrounding the brain. If hydrocephalus is left untreated, the condition can lead to head enlargement and severe brain damage. Medical doctors usually treat hydrocephalus by a surgical insertion of a shunt, which is a one way valve that diverts the cerebrospinal fluid away from the brain and into the blood stream. These shunts sometimes fall out of place and replacement is necessary as the child grows older. Even if the shunt does not fall out of place, it must be replaced periodically as the child grows older. Teachers who work with children having shunts should be aware that blockage, disconnection, or infection of the shunt could result in increased introcranial pressure. We have been told by experts that some of the warning signs of the disconnection are drowsiness, vomiting, headache, irritability, and squinting. These things should be heeded in a child with a shunt because they can be life threatening.

MUSCULAR DYSTROPHY

Muscular dystrophy refers to a group of long-term diseases that progressively weaken and waste away the body's muscle. As a matter of fact, the body's muscles are replaced with fatty tissue. The most common form is buchenne muscular dystrophy which affects boys much more frequently than girls. The child appears normal at birth, but muscle weakness usually occurs between the ages of two and six. One of the first signs is weakness that the child may experience in running or climbing stairs. The child may also walk with an unusual gait which is often referred to as a duck-like gait. The calf muscles of a child with muscular dystrophy may appear unusually large because the degenerated muscle has been replaced by fatty tissue.

Children with muscular dystrophy often have difficulty getting to their feet after lying down or while they have been playing on the floor. These children easily fall, and by the age of 10 to 14, the child loses the ability to walk. The small muscles of the hands and fingers are usually the last to be affected and some doctors and therapists recommend the early use of electrically powered wheelchairs for these children. Others suggest employing special braces; another advice is to prolong walking as long as possible.

There is no known cure for most of the cases of muscular dystrophy and the disease is often fatal. If the child receives regular physical therapy, a good deal of independence can be maintained. The teacher may also need to help the child deal with the gradual loss of physical abilities and maybe the possibility of death.

OSTEOGENESIS IMPERFECTA

Osteogenesis imperfecta is a rare inherited condition that is marked by extremely brittle bones. The skeletal system does not grow normally and the bones are easily fractured. The children who have this condition are fragile and must be protected. Wheelchairs are usually necessary and, although the child may be able to walk a short distance with the aid of braces or protective equipment, the wheelchair is still needed. Like other children with orthopedic impairments, the child with osteogenesis imperfecta may have frequent hospitalizations and may even need surgery. As children mature, their bones often become less brittle and they often require less attention.

TRAUMATIC BRAIN INJURY

Injuries to the head are common in children and adults. The number one cause of head injuries is automobile accidents and most head injuries occur in adolescence. It is predicted that each year one in 500 school age children will be hospitalized with traumatic head injuries. The other

significant causes of head trauma besides the automobile, include motor-
cycle and bicycle accidents, falls, assaults, gunshot wounds, and child
abuse. Severe head trauma often results in a coma which is an abnormal
deep stupor from which it is often impossible to arouse the affected
individual. Temporary or lasting symptoms may include cognitive language disability, memory loss, seizures, and perceptual disorders. The
educational and lifelong needs of students with head injuries will depend
on the amount of brain damage that has been done and whether the
child's intelligence is affected or not.

When it was originally passed, the IDEA did not specifically mention
children with head trauma. However, when the law was amended in
1990 (PL 101-476), traumatic brain injury was added as a new disability
category. Many children with head injuries will have on-going health
problems such as paralysis, chronic fatigue, headaches, and seizures;
therefore, they are served under the category Other Health Impaired.
Tyler and Mira (1993) suggest several modifications that teachers
may want to make in order to assist students with a traumatic head
injury:

- A shortened school day, concentrating academic instruction during peak
  performance periods, frequent breaks, and a reduced class load may be
  necessitated by the chronic fatigue that some students with head injury
  experience for a year or more.
- A special resource period at the beginning and end of each school day when a
  teacher, counselor, or aide helps the student plan or review the day's schedule,
  keep track of assignments, and monitor progress may be required because of
  problems with loss of memory and organization.
- Modifications such as an extra set of textbooks at home, a peer to help the
  student move efficiently from class to class, and early dismissal from class
  to allow time to get to the next room can help the student who has difficulties
  with mobility, balance, or coordination (adaptive physical education is often
  indicated).
- Behavior management and/or counseling interventions may be needed to
  help with problems such as poor judgment, impulsiveness, overactivity,
  aggression, destructiveness, and socially uninhibited behavior often experienced by students with head injury.
- Modifications of instruction and testing procedures such as tape-recording
  lectures, assigning a note taker, and allowing extra time to take tests may be
  needed.
- IEP goals and objectives may need to be reviewed and modified as often as
  every 30 days because of the dramatic changes in behavior and performance
  by some children during the early stages of recovery.

CEREBRAL PALSY

Cerebral palsy is a disability that always is caused by damage to the brain. This damage can occur before, during, or after birth. It is often evidenced by motor problems, general physical weakness, lack of coordination, and speech disorders. This syndrome is not contagious, progressive, or remittent. The seriousness of this condition ranges from mild to very severe. Tables 2.1 and 2.2 show the focus on motor and topographical characteristics. The motor scheme emphasizes the type and nature of physiological involvement or impairment. The topographical scheme focuses on the various body parts or limbs which are affected.

Table 2.1
Motor Classification for Cerebral Palsy

Classification	Brief Description
Spasticity	Characterized by great difficulty in using muscles for movement; involuntary contractions occur with attempts to stretch or use various muscle groups; spasticity prevents performance of controlled, voluntary motions.
Athetosis	Characterized by constant contorted twisting motions, particularly in the wrists and fingers; facial contortions are also common; continual movement and contraction of successive muscle groups prevents any well-controlled use of muscular motion.
Ataxia	Characterized by extreme difficulties in controlling both gross and fine motor movements; problems related to balance, position in space, and directionality make coordinated movement extremely difficult if not impossible.
Rigidity	Characterizes one of the most severe and rare types of cerebral palsy; involves continuous and diffuse tension as the limbs are extended; walking or movement of any type is extremely difficult.
Tremor	Characterized by motions that are constant, involuntary, and uncontrollable; are of a rhythmic, alternating, or pendular pattern and result from muscle contractions that occur continuously.
Atonia	Characterized by little if any muscle tone; muscles fail to respond to any stimulation; condition is extremely rare in its true form.
Mixed	Characterized by combinations of all the conditions described above.

Table 2.2
Topographical Classification of Cerebral Palsy and Paralytic Condition

Classification	Affected Area
Monoplegia	One limb
Paraplegia	Lower body and both legs
Hemiplegia	One side of the body
Triplegia	Three appendages or limbs, usually both legs and one arm
Quadriplegia	All four extremities and usually the trunk
Diplegia	Legs are more involved than arms
Double hemiplegia	Both halves of the body, with one side more involved than the other.

Causation and Prevalence

The causes of cerebral palsy are many. Any condition that can adversely affect the brain may cause cerebral palsy. The individual with cerebral palsy is likely to have mild to severe problems in nonmotor areas of functioning as well as motor areas. These difficulties often include hearing impairments, speech and language disorders, intellectual deficits, visual impairments, and general perceptual problems.

It has been found that 40 percent of cerebral palsy children have average or above average intelligence. Sixty percent have IQs below average and many of them fall into the moderate and profound range of retardation.

The prevalence of cerebral palsy ranges from 1.5 per 1,000 live births. These figures fluctuate from time to time. For example, many children born with cerebral palsy come from families who are unable to obtain medical care; therefore, these children don't go to physicians and the prevalence is not reported. As the families gain financial help through Medicare, Medicaid, or because of work, they may go to a physician later on and the case is then reported.

CONVULSIVE DISORDERS (EPILEPSY)

Experts in the field tell us that anyone can have a seizure, which is a disturbance of movement, sensation, behavior, and/or consciousness caused by abnormal activity in the brain. It is not uncommon for seizures to occur if one has a high fever, drinks excessive alcohol, or experiences a blow to the head. Most of the onsets of epilepsy or convulsive disorder occur before the age of five or after the age of 60. When seizures occur chronically and repeatedly, however, the condition is known as a convulsive disorder, or as most people call the condition, epilepsy. With proper medical treatment and the support of parents, teachers, and peers, many students with convulsive disorders have full and normal lives. Most of the students with epilepsy have normal intelligence. Many of them can go full time to the regular classroom for their education. Occasionally, though, students miss so much of the instruction during the day because of petit mal seizures that they must have special education help.

Epileptic seizures may be largely controlled by anticonvulsant medications. Some children require such heavy doses, though, that their learning and behavior are seriously affected and some medications have undesirable side effects such as drowsiness, nausea, and weight gain.

The specific causes of epilepsy are not known, but it is believed that people become seizure prone when a particular area of the brain becomes electrically unstable. This condition may result because of an underlying lesion caused by scar tissue from a head injury. It could also be caused by scar tissue from a tumor or an interruption in blood supply to the brain. In many cases, the origin of seizure activity is never traced to a particular instance. A convulsive disorder can occur at any stage during one's life. There is a wide variety of psychological, physical, and sensory factors that trigger seizures in susceptible people. Some examples are fatigue, excitement, anger, surprise, bright lights, alcohol or drugs, or a loud sound.

During a seizure, there is a dysfunction in the electrochemical activity of the brain and this causes a person to lose control of his muscles temporarily. Between seizures, which is most of the time, the brain functions normally.

There are several types of seizures, but three of them are relatively common. The generalized tonic/clonic seizure which was once called grand mal is the most serious type of convulsive disorder. A generalized tonic/clonic seizure can be disturbing and frightening to someone who has never seen one. It can also be disturbing and frightening to someone who has seen one before. The affected child generally has no warning that a seizure is about to occur, but the muscles become stiff and the child loses consciousness and falls to the floor. The entire body shakes violently as the muscles alternately contract and relax. Saliva is often forced from the mouth, the legs and arms may jerk, and the bladder and bowels are often emptied. After about two to five minutes, the contractions diminish and the child goes to sleep or regains consciousness in a confused or drowsy state. Generalized tonic/chronic seizures may occur several times during a day or as seldom as once or twice a year. They are more likely to occur during the day than at night. Approximately 80 percent of children can be free of seizures with medication.

The absence seizure, which was previously called the petit mal, is less serious than the grand mal seizure, but often is more frequent. Sometimes the absence seizure occurs as many as 100 times per day. There is generally a brief loss of consciousness lasting anywhere from a few seconds to a half minute or a minute. The child may stare blankly, flutter or blink his eyes, grow pale, his arm and hand may twitch, and he may drop whatever he is holding. Sometimes a teacher mistakenly thinks this child is daydreaming or not listening. The child may or may not be aware that he had a seizure, but nothing special is necessary for this type child.

A complex/partial seizure which used to be called a psychomotor seizure may appear as a brief period of inappropriate activity. The child may smack his lips, walk around aimlessly, or shout things that don't make sense. He may actually start picking up clothes and throwing them out of the dirty clothes hamper, or he could just start touching the floor and talking extremely fast. Complex/partial seizures generally last from two to five minutes after which the child has amnesia about the whole episode.

A simple/partial seizure is characterized by a sudden jerking motion with no loss of consciousness. Partial seizures may occur daily, weekly, monthly, or only once or twice a year. The teacher should keep dangerous objects out of the child's way and not try to restrain a child having any type of seizure.

Some children experience a warning sensation called an aura a short time before a seizure. The aura is actually the beginning of a seizure and seldom can a seizure be stopped because the aura has taken place. The aura takes different forms in different people. Some people have distinctive feelings, sights, sounds, and tastes; even smells are described by some children. The aura can be a safety valve which allows the child to leave the class before the seizure actually occurs.

DIABETES

Juvenile diabetes mellitus is a disorder of metabolism. It affects the way the body absorbs or breaks down the sugars and starches in foods. Diabetes is a common childhood disease which affects about one in 600 school-age children, so we can be fairly sure that most teachers will encounter students with diabetes. Without proper medical management, the diabetic child's system is not able to obtain and retain adequate energy from food. The cells actually starve in the diabetic child if he cannot absorb the glucose from the food. Not only does the child lack energy, but many important parts of the body such as the eyes and the kidneys can be affected by untreated diabetes. Early symptoms of diabetes include excessive thirst, excessive urination, headaches, weight loss in spite of a good appetite, and cuts that are slow to heal. Children with diabetes have insufficient insulin which is a hormone that is produced by the pancreas and is necessary for proper metabolism and digestion of foods. To regulate the condition, insulin must be injected daily under the skin. Most children with diabetes learn to inject their own insulin, and sometimes as often as three or four times a day. Children with diabetes also must follow a specific diet prescribed by a physician or nutrition specialist.

Teachers should be aware of the symptoms of insulin reaction, also called diabetic shock. It can result from taking too much insulin, which is sometimes caused by strenuous exercise or a missed or delayed meal. The blood sugar level is lowered by insulin and exercise allayed by food. Some of the symptoms of insulin reaction include faintness, dizziness, blurred vision, drowsiness, and nausea. A child often appears irritable and seems to have a marked personality change. In many cases, giving the child some form of concentrated sugar such as a glass of fruit juice or a candy bar ends the insulin reaction in a few minutes. The child's doctor or parent should inform the teacher and school health personnel of appropriate foods to give the child in case of insulin reaction; teachers often don't know that a diabetic coma is more serious. If the child has too little insulin, he can go into a diabetic coma. If food is given then, it could cause serious effects in the child and even death. The symptoms of diabetic coma include fatigue; thirst; dry, hot skin; excessive urination; and labored breathing. If the teacher suspects that the child is in a diabetic coma, a doctor or nurse should be called immediately.

If the child does not have enough insulin, he or she can develop hyperglycemia (too much sugar), also known as ketoacidosis. If insulin is not administered, the individual will fall into a diabetic coma. Sometimes the person appears to be drunk. The treatment, of course, is insulin. Stress, eating too many carbohydrates, illness, and forgetting to take insulin can all cause hyperglycemia.

At the other end of the spectrum is hypoglycemia or not enough sugar. Increased physical activity, as already stated, taking too much insulin, or not eating enough can cause the person to have too much insulin. Insulin shock or insulin reaction often occurs before meal time, especially if the meal is delayed.

CYSTIC FIBROSIS

Cystic fibrosis is a genetically transmitted disease of children and adolescents. The body's exocrine glands excrete a thick mucus that often blocks the lungs and parts of the digestive system. It is an inherited disease that is transmitted through a recessive gene; therefore, both parents must have the recessive gene. Children with cystic fibrosis often have difficulty breathing and are susceptible to many pulmonary infections. Malnutrition and poor growth are common characteristics of children with cystic fibrosis because the pancreas is not working adequately. When the pancreas doesn't work adequately, it causes an inadequate digestion and malabsorption of nutrients, especially fats. These children often have large and frequent bowel movements which smell very bad.

The average life expectancy of individuals today who have cystic fibrosis is 29 years. The life expectancy has increased substantially over the years.

Medications are prescribed for children with cystic fibrosis which include enzymes to facilitate digestion and solutions to thin and loosen the mucus found in the lungs. Sometimes during physical exercises some children may need help from teachers to clear their lungs and air passages.

HEMOPHILIA

Hemophilia is a rare hereditary disorder that affects approximately 70,000 people in the United States. It is a disorder in which the blood does not clot as quickly as it should. The most serious consequences are usually internal bleeding. Generally, minor cuts and scrapes do not cause serious problems. Internal bleeding, however, can cause swelling, pain, and permanent damage to joints, tissues, and internal organs. Often this child must be hospitalized for blood transfusions. It is thought that emotional stress may intensify episodes. A student with hemophilia may need to be excused from some physical activities and may use a wheelchair during periods of susceptibility. This condition is generally found in America among African-Americans or people from Indian ancestry. This does not include the Native American Indians, but people from the country of India.

REFERENCES

Byers, J. (1989). AIDS in children: Effects on neurological development and implications for the future. *The Journal of Special Education, 23*(1), 5–16.

Heward, W. L. (1995). *Exceptional children (5th ed.)*. Columbus, OH: Prentice-Hall.

National Heart, Lung, and Blood Institute. (1992). *Data fact sheet.* Bethesda, MD: U.S. Department of Health and Human Services.

Paul, G. H., & Fafoglia, B. A. (1988). *All about asthma and how to live with it.* New York: Sterling.

Turnbull, A. F., Turnbull, H. R., Shank, M., & Leal, D. (1985). *Exceptional lives.* Englewood Cliffs, NJ: Merrill/Prentice-Hall.

Tyler, J. S., & Mira, M. P. (1993). Educational modifications for students with head injuries. *Teaching Exceptional Children, 25*(3), 24–27.

Chapter 3

MENTAL RETARDATION

E ducators have always known that some children learn more slowly than others and they have difficulty adapting to social and educational demands of their age mates. About two hundred years ago, an organized attempt to educate the mentally retarded took place when Jean Marc Itard, a French physician, attempted to educate a young boy found wandering in the woods. The boy was dubbed The Wild Boy of Aveyron because of the name of the forest in which he was found that is located in Southern France. The boy was given the name Victor and Itard worked with him on a daily basis in an attempt to educate him. Although Itard achieved only a few of his objectives, one of his students, Edward Seguin, later developed and published in book form Itard's approaches. Seguin also became an acknowledged leader of the movement to educate mentally retarded children and adults.

In 1848, political turmoil forced Seguin to leave France and come to the United States. His work in the U.S. helped move mentally retarded children toward a better education and a happier life. Gradually, the mentally retarded moved from institutions to the public schools and within the public schools to the least restrictive environment.

Educators have identified three levels of mental retardation—mild, moderate, and severe and profound. In this chapter we shall discuss mild retardation and the upper limits of moderate.

Definition

The most common definition of mental retardation was devised by the American Association on Mental Retardation (AAMR):

Mental retardation refers to significantly sub-average general intellectual functioning existing concurrently with deficits in adaptive behavior and manifested during the developmental period" (Grossman, 1983, p. 1). Kirk, Gallagher, and Anastasiow (1993) have this to say about that definition: "What do these words mean? Significantly subaverage general intellectual functioning" is often considered a score on a standard intelligence test lower than that obtained by 97 to 98 percent

50

of people the same age. "Deficits in adaptive behavior" is the person's failure to meet standards of independence and social responsibility expected of his or her age and cultural group. The "developmental period" is the time from birth to age 18. A child with mental retardation, then, scores in the lowest 2 or 3 percent of his or her age group on an intelligence test, has problems learning basic academic skills, and is not adapting well to his or her surroundings (p. 166).

Intellectual Subnormality

A definition, no matter how comprehensive, means very little unless we can take the abstractions and translate them into something that we can all understand. We know that mentally retarded children are slower than their age mates in reasoning, using memory, associating and classifying information, and in making sound judgments. These are the types of performances which are measured on intelligence tests.

According to Grossman (1983), the ranges for mild, moderate, and severe retardation are as follows:

Level of Retardation	I.Q. Score
Mild	50–55 to 70
Moderate	35–40 to 50–55
Severe and Profound	lower than 35

Adaptive Behavior

The AAMR definition emphasizes the role of adaptive behavior in determining whether a person is retarded. A child can score low on a standardized intelligence test but have adequate adaptive skills; he or she may do poorly in school but still be "streetwise"—able to cope, for example, with the subway system, with an after school job or with peers. Much of the AAMR definition's emphasis on adaptive behavior can be traced to the 1970 report on the President's Committee on Mental Retardation entitled "The Six-Hour Retarded Child." It held that while some children may function in the retarded range in school for six hours of the day, they behave normally—adjust and adapt competently—once they return to the home community for the other eighteen hours.

Adaptive behavior is more than the ability to survive outside school. Adaptive skills are age- and situation-specific. They are different for the preschooler and the adult. The inner-city teenager may need to be streetwise, but the teenager in a rural community requires a very different set of abilities. The AAMR specifies that in infancy and early childhood, sensorimotor, communication, self-help, and socialization skills are important. In middle childhood and early adolescence, adaptive behavior makes use of abilities involving learning processes and interpersonal social skills. In late adolescence and adulthood, vocational skills and social responsibilities are of utmost importance.

Intellectual Functioning

The words "subaverage general intellectual functioning" in the AAMR definition refer to scores more than two standard deviations below the mean on a standardized test of intelligence. One commonly used IQ is the Wechsler Intelligence Scale for Children—3 (WISC-3). On this test, a score of 70 would be two standard deviations below the mean, or average, of 100.

The Stanford-Binet has a standard deviation of 16; therefore, 32 minus 100 (mean IQ of people in U.S.) equals sixty-eight (68). If we use the Stanford-Binet mental retardation begins at IQ 68. In the AAMR manual, however, it states that a cutoff of 75 might be warranted as the beginning of mental retardation in some cases.

Prevalence

The average or mean score on an IQ test is 100. Theoretically, we expect 2.27 percent of the population to fall two standard deviations (IQ = 70 on the WISC-3) or more below this average. This expectation is based on the assumption that intelligence, like so many other human traits, is distributed along a "normal curve." Figure 3.1 shows the hypothetical normal curve of intelligence. This curve is split into eight areas by means of standard deviations. On the WISC-3, where one standard deviation equals 15 IQ points, 34.13 percent of the population scores between 85 and 100. Likewise, 2.14 percent scores between 55 and 70, and 0.13 percent scores below 55. Thus it would seem that 2.27 percent should fall between 0 and 70.

In keeping with the figure of 2.27, the U.S. government for years estimated the prevalence of retardation to be 2.3 percent. The U.S. Department of Education (1989), however, has reported that for 1987–88, 1.21 percent of the population from six to seventeen years of age was identified as mentally retarded by the public schools. Authorities have pointed to three possible sources for discrepancy between 2.3 and 1.21 percent. First, the fact that retarded children must now meet the dual criteria of low IQ *and* low adaptive behavior may have resulted in fewer children being identified. Second, litigation focusing on the improper labeling of minority students as mentally retarded may have made school

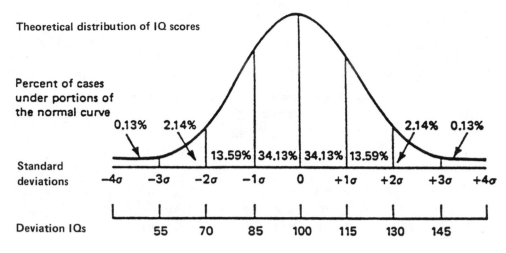

Figure 3.1. Theoretical distribution of IQ scores based on normal curve.

personnel more cautious about identifying these children as retarded. Third, parents and school officials are more likely to label children as learning disabled rather than mentally retarded because it is perceived as a less stigmatizing label.

Kirk Gallagher and Anastasiow (1993) state that:

> Strict adherence to an IQ score of 70 as a cutoff point probably accounts for much of the reduced prevalence of mental retardation in the public schools. It also affects our description of mild mental retardation. The characteristics of the group of mildly retarded children change as the boundaries of the population change (p. 171).

Causes

Most experts estimate that we are able to pinpoint the cause of mental retardation in about 6–15 percent of the cases. Generally speaking, the set of casual factors for mild retardation differs from that for more severe levels of retardation.

Mild Retardation

Most people identified as retarded are classified as mildly retarded. They typically don't look any different from the nonhandicapped population and they are seldom diagnosed as mentally retarded until they enter school. Although we can't definitely pinpoint the cause of mild retardation, Heber (1959) stated that the cultural-familial retarded person was one who had (1) no evidence of brain damage, (2) at least one parent who was retarded, and (3) at least one retarded sibling (if he or she had siblings). The assumption was that the retardation was due to genetic or social-environmental factors.

More recently the term has come to be used when it is suspected that the retardation is caused by poor social-environmental conditions rather than heredity. Thus most professionals believe that a culturally-familially retarded person is one who (1) is mildly retarded, (2) has no evidence of brain damage, and (3) is being or has been raised in poor social-environmental conditions. Social-environmental conditions are presumed to cause the retardation because they produce such effects as inadequate learning opportunities and nutrition. But because these effects are difficult to pinpoint as causes, the classification of cultural-familial retardation tends to serve as a broad and rather vague catchall category—actually a "pseudo-casual" category. When authorities refer to the large numbers of retarded persons for whom no cause can be determined, most of the individuals they are talking about have been classified as culturally-familially retarded.

The Nature versus Nurture Controversy

How much of an individual's intelligence is determined by environmental factors and how much of it is decided by genetic makeup? This is one of the oldest debates in the fields of special education and psychology, and it will probably continue indefinitely. In the early part of this century, proponents of the viewpoint that genetics determines intellectual development largely held sway. The classic study of Skeels and Dye (1930), however, did much to strengthen the position of the environmentalists. Skeels and Dye investigated the effects of stimulation on the development of infants and young children, many of whom were classified as mentally retarded, in an orphanage. One group of children remained in the typical orphanage environment, whereas the other group was given stimulation. For the later group, nurturance was provided by retarded teenage girls who were institutionalized. The effects were clear-cut: Average IQs for members of the group given stimulation increased, whereas the other children's IQs decreased. Even more dramatic were the results of Skeel's follow-up study, done twenty-one years later:

> In the adult follow-up study, all cases were located and information obtained on them, after a lapse of 21 years.
> All 13 children in the experimental group were self-supporting, and none was

a ward of any institution. . . . In the contrast group of 12 children, one had died in adolescence following continued residence in a state institution for the mentally retarded, and four were still wards of institutions, one in a mental hospital, and the other three in institutions for the mentally retarded.

In education, disparity between the two groups was striking. The contrast group completed a median of less than the third grade. The experimental group completed a median of the 12th grade. Four of the subjects had one or more years of college work, one received a B.A. degree and took some graduate training.

Marked differences in occupational levels were seen in the two groups. In the experimental group, all were self-supporting or married and functioning as housewives. The range was from professional and business occupations to domestic service, the latter the occupations of two girls who had never been placed in adoptive homes. In the contrast group, four (36 percent) of the subjects were institutionalized and unemployed. Those who were employed, with one exception, were characterized as "hewers of wood and drawers of water." . . .

Eleven of the 13 children in the experimental group were married: nine of the 11 had a total of 28 children, an average of three per family. On intelligence tests, these second generation children had IQs ranging from 86 to 125, with a mean of 104. In no instance was there any indication of mental retardation or demonstrable abnormality. . . .

In the contrast group, only two subjects had married. One had one child and subsequently was divorced. Psychological examination of the child revealed marked mental retardation. . . . Another male subject had a nice home and a family of four children, all of average intelligence. (Skeels, 1966, pp. 54–55)

By the 1960s, there was a large number of proponents of the nurture position. It was during this time, for example, that the U.S. government established the Head Start program. Head Start was based on the premise that the negative effects of poverty could be reduced through educational and medical services during the preschool years.

By the 1980s most authorities believed that both genetics and environment are critical determinants of intelligence. They arrived at this judgment on the basis of several studies, but one of the most convincing was that conducted by Capron and Duyme (1989), who compared the IQs of four groups of adopted children: (1) children whose biological and adoptive parents were both of high socioeconomic status (SES), (2) children whose biological parents were of high SES but whose adoptive parents were of low SES, (3) children whose biological and adoptive parents were both of low SES, and (4) children whose biological parents were of low SES but whose adoptive parents were of high SES. The average IQs of the four groups were 119.60, 107.50, 92.40, and 103.60, respectively. Confirming the importance of the environment, the average IQ of the adoptees was about 12 points higher (111.60 versus 99.95) when they were raised by parents of high (groups 1 and 4) rather than low SES (groups 2 and 3). Confirming the importance of heredity, the average IQ of the adoptees was about 16 points higher (113.55 versus 98.00) when their biological parents were of high SES (groups 1 and 2) compared to low SES (groups 3 and 4).

The more scientists study genetic and environmental determinants of intelligence, the more they realize how complex the influence of these factors is. For example, scientists are far from being able to specify the exact way in which the environment influences intellectual development. They do say, however, that genetics are just as important as environment.

Did you know that, in the United States . . . ? *

- More than 0.5 million students with mental retardtion attend public schools.

- The number of students with mental retardation served in the public schools has declined steadily since 1977. (There are several explanations for this decline, including the preferences of parents and professionals to use labels such as *learning disabled* or *developmentally disabled* rather than *mentally retarded.*

- Although more than 50,000 special education teachers currently work with students who are mentally retarded, 4,000 more are still needed.

- The number of special education teachers employed to work with students who are mentally retarded is second only to the number of teachers who work with students with learning disabilities.

- The vast majority (69 percent) of students with mental retardation are served in separate special education classes and schools.

Did you know that, worldwide. . . ? **

- There are more than 300 million people with mental retardation.

- Mental retardation is more than 7 times as prevalent as blindness or deafness; 10 times as prevalent as physical disabilities; and 12 times as prevalent as cerebral palsy.

- Mental retardation is approximately two to three times as prevalent in the nations of Africa, Asia, and Latin America as in the United States.

Sources:
*Joseph P. Kennedy, Jr., Foundation. (1991). *Facts about mental retardation.* Washington, DC: Author. Adapted.
**From U.S. Department of Education, 1991.

Figure 3.2. Think about this.

There are many things about the mentally retarded that people, including teachers, don't know. Figure 3.2 tells us some things about the mentally retarded that are not common knowledge.

Causes of Mental Retardation

Mental retardation is often classified on the basis of the origin of the condition rather than the severity or educational expectations associated with it. A classification system that uses the cause or etiology of the condition to differentiate retarded individuals is often referred to as a medical classification system because it originated in the field of medicine. The most commonly used medical descriptor system is that from the AAMR (Grossman, 1983), which uses the following ten categories:

1. Infection and intoxication (e.g., syphilis, rubella)
2. Trauma or a physical agent (e.g., injury during birth, prenatal injury)
3. Nutritional or metabolic disorders (e.g., PKU, thyroid dysfunction)
4. Gross postnatal brain disease (e.g., tuberous sclerosis)
5. Diseases and conditions resulting from unknown prenatal influences (e.g., hydrocephalus)
6. Chromasomal abnormalities (e.g., Down syndrome)
7. Gestational disorders (e.g., prematurity)
8. Psychiatric disorders
9. Environmental influences (e.g., sensory deprivation, social disadvantage)
10. Other conditions (e.g., unknown causes or such known causes as blindness or deafness)

Ih Figure 3.3 the reader can readily see that many myths abound about the mentally retarded person. The author discounts the myths with the facts.

Causation

Mental retardation is the result of multiple causes, some known, many unknown. The possible causes of mental retardation include sociocultural differences, infection and intoxication, chromosomal abnormalities, gestation disorders, unknown prenatal influences, traumas or physical agents, metabolic or nutritional factors, and postnatal brain disease.

Sociocultural Influences. Westling (1986) stated, "Poor people have poor nutritional characteristics" (p. 100). MacMillan (1982) further explained that the highest prevalence of mental retardation occurs among

"people referred to as culturally deprived, culturally different, or culturally disadvantaged, or some other term that denotes adverse economic and living conditions. Children of high risk are those who live in slums, and frequently, who are members of certain ethnic minorities groups. In these high risk groups there is poor medical care for mother and child, the high rate of broken families, and little value for education or motivation to achieve" (pp. 86–87).

Myth	Fact
Once diagnosed as mentally retarded, a person remains within this classification for the rest of his or her life.	The level of mental functioning does not necessarily remain stable, particularly for those in the mild classification.
If a person achieves a low score on an IQ test, this means that his or her adaptive skills are also sure to be subnormal.	It is possible for a person to have a tested subnormal IQ and still have adequate adaptive skills. Much depends on the individual's training, motivation, experience, social environment, etc.
Children with Down syndrome are always happy, compliant, and pleasant to have around.	In general, although they are often tractable and good-natured, the idea that they are significantly more so than other children is exaggerated.
Retarded individuals go through different learning stages compared to nonhandicapped indiiduals.	Studies indicate that the learning characteristics of retarded individuals, particularly those classified as mildly retarded, do not differ from those of nonhandicapped people. Retarded people go through the same stages, but at a slower rate.
Children classified as moderately retarded (once called "trainable") require a radically different curriculum from that appropriate for children classified as mildly retarded (once called "educable").	Although academic subjects are generally stressed more in classes for the mildly retarded, this generalization does not always hold true for individual children.
Most mental retardation can be diagnosed in infancy.	Most children eventually diagnosed as retarded are not so identified until they go to school.
Most mentally retarded children look different from nonhandicapped children.	The vast majority of mentally retarded children are mildly retarded, and most mildly retarded children look like nonhandicapped children.
In most cases, the cause of retardation can be identified.	In most cases (especially within the mild classification), the cause cannot be identified. For many of the children in the mild classification, it is thought that poor environment may be a causal factor. However, it is usully extremely difficult to document.
Severely retarded people are helpless.	With appropriate educational programming, many severely retarded people can lead relatively independent lives. In fact, with appropriate professional support, some can live in the community and even enter competitive employment.

Figure 3.3. Myths and facts about mentally retarded individuals.

The author has already discussed the study by Skeels and Dye which dealt with nature vs. nurture. Numerous studies over the years have focused on the degree to which both heredity and environment contribute to intelligence. What has been learned from these studies is that, while there is a better understanding of the interactive effects of both heredity and environment, the exact contribution of each to intellectual growth remains somewhat unknown. Recent evidence, though, does indicate that at least heredity is as important as is environment and we can safely say that 50 percent can be attributed to heredity and 50 percent to environment.

The term to describe children whose retardation may be attributable to both sociocultural and genetic factors is cultural-familial. These people are often described as (1) being mildly retarded, (2) having no known biological cause for the condition, (3) having at least one parent or sibling who is also mildly retarded, and (4) growing up in a low socioeconomic level home environment.

We know that for the majority of individuals, moderate, severe, and profound retardation problems are evident at birth. The American Association on Mental Retardation has grouped the causes of mental retardation into several categories (Grossman, 1983). In order for the reader to gain a greater understanding of the diversity of causes associated with mental retardation, those categories are briefly discussed here.

Infection and Intoxication. Several types of maternal infection may result in difficulties for the fetus or unborn child. The probability for damage is very high if infection occurs during the first three months of pregnancy as in congenital rubella or German measles. Rubella is a viral infection which causes a variety of problems, including mental retardation, blindness, deafness, cerebral palsy, heart problems, seizures, and other neurological problems.

Another infection with which we associate mental retardation is syphilis. Syphilis transmitted from the mother to the unborn child can result in severe birth defects. With syphilis, bacteria actually crosses the placenta and infects the fetus. The result is damage to the central nervous system as well as to the circulatory system.

Several prenatal infections can cause serious disorders. For example, toxoplasmosis is an infection that is carried by raw meat and fecal material. The damage from toxoplasmosis can be significant and can result in mental retardation and blindness and convulsions. Toxoplasmosis is primarily a threat if the mother is exposed during pregnancy.

Intoxication refers to cerebral damage that occurs due to an excessive level of some toxic agent in the mother/fetus system. The excessive use of alcohol by the mother or excessive use of drugs can cause damage to the fetus. Other environmental hazards such as X-rays or insecticides may also cause damage to the child. Damage to the fetus that is caused by the maternal alcohol consumption is known as fetal alcohol syndrome.

This condition is characterized by facial abnormalities, heart problems, low birth weight, and mental retardation. It is estimated that more than 50,000 children are born with alcohol-related problems each year in the United States (National Association, 1991). Prescription drugs such as anticonvulsants and antibiotics have also been associated with infant malformation (Batshaw & Perret, 1986).

Another factor that can cause mental retardation is an incompatible blood type between the mother and the fetus. The most widely known form of this problem is when the mother's blood is Rh negative and the fetus' blood is Rh positive. In this situation, the mother's system may become sensitized to the incompatible blood type and produce antibodies that damage the fetus. Medical technology can prevent this condition through the use of a drug called Rhogam®.

Mental retardation can also be caused as a result of postnatal infections and toxic excesses. For example, encephalitis may damage the central nervous system following certain types of childhood infection, for example, measles or mumps. Reaction to certain toxic substances such as lead, carbon monoxide, and certain antibiotics can also cause central nervous system damage.

Chromosomal Abnormalities. The chromosomes of our body are threadlike agents that carry the genes which play the critical role in determining inherited characteristics. Defects resulting from chromosomal abnormalities are typically traumatic. They are often severe and are accompanied by visually evident abnormalities. Fortunately, genetically-caused defects are relatively rare. The vast majority of humans have normal cell structure, and development proceeds without undue accidents. The human body cells normally have 46 chromosomes which are arranged in 23 pairs. If we have an aberration in chromosomal arrangement, either before fertilization or during early cell division, damage may result in a variety of ways.

One of the most widely recognized types of mental retardation, Down syndrome, results from chromosomal abnormalities. Down syndrome is a condition that results in facial and physical characteristics which are visably quite distinctive. The facial features are marked by distinctive epicanthic eyefolds, prominent cheek bones, and a small somewhat flattened nose. About 5 percent of individuals who have mental retardation have Down syndrome.

Down syndrome has received wide-spread attention in the literature and has been a topic in medical and special education textbooks for many years. Part of this attention has come about because of the apparent ability to identify a cause with a great deal of certainty. The cause of such genetic errors has become increasingly associated with the ages of both the father and the mother. MacMillan (1982) reported that, for mothers between the ages of 20 and 30, the chances of having a child with Down syndrome is one in 1,200. This increases to one in 20 for mothers older than 45 years of age. Other authors (Abroms & Bennett) indicated that about one in 25 percent of the cases associated with Trisomy 21, the age of the father is also a factor, and this is particularly true if he is over 55 years old.

According to current figures, more than 50 percent of children with Down syndrome are born to mothers older than 35. Scientists have not found out exactly why age is related to the condition. We do know, however, that the mother is not the exclusive source as already mentioned of the extra chromosome. A father contributes the extra chromosome in 20–25 percent of all cases.

Down syndrome can also be caused by a chromosomal abnormality, called *translocation*. The child may have 46 chromosomes, but one pair breaks and the broken part fuses to another chromosome. The incidence of Down syndrome is one to two of 1,000 births. Before the 1970s, the diagnosis of Down syndrome and several other pathological conditions was not made until the child was born or even later. Amniocentesis, which is a procedure for drawing a sample of amniotic fluid that surrounds the fetus in the uterus from the pregnant woman, has made earlier diagnosis possible. Fetal cells in the fluid are analyzed for chromosomal abnormality by karyotyping which is a process in which a picture of chromosomal patterns is prepared. Tests of prenatal maternal alpha-fetoprotein and ultrasonography can also reveal the presence of a fetus with Down syndrome, which has posed a major dilemma for the families and doctors. This early diagnosis allows the parents to decide whether the pregnancy should be terminated. The decision is not an easy one and generates many problems.

The effect of Down syndrome extends well beyond the child's early development. Research shows that persons with Down syndrome are at substantial risk in later years for Alzheimer's and dementia.

Phenylketonuria. Phenylketonuria is an inborn error of metabolism. Normal growth and development in the embryo and fetus depends on the production of enzymes at the right time and place. When the enzymes are not produced or fail to perform their normal functions, a number of problems and conditions can result. A single gene defect that can produce severe retardation is phenylketonuria. In PKU, the absence of a specific enzyme in the liver leads to a build up of the amino acid phenylalanine.

The effects of PKU and other metabolic disorders such as hyperthyroidism can be controlled by modifying the child's nutritional intake. Such modifications, though, must begin in infancy if they are to help. Fortunately, the conditions can be detected in the newborn's blood. Today, all 50 states screen for PKU and hyperthyroidism at birth and about 20 states screen for other metabolic disorders as well.

TOXIC AGENTS

The woman has a remarkable system whereby she transmits nutrients through the umbilical cord to her fetus. Unfortunately, this is also a highway by which many damaging substances can pass through to the developing fetus. Medical science has made it fairly easy to monitor fetal development and the rapidly growing body of research from studies of animals has raised concerns about the effects on the unborn child of certain substances taken into the body by the expectant mother. The word teratogen, which comes from the Greek, meaning monster, is a substance that adversely affects fetal development. Drugs, which include alcohol or cigarette smoke, are prime examples of a teratogen. Also, another prime example would be contaminated air that we breathe.

Fetal Alcohol Syndrome. The heavy use of alcohol by pregnant women often results in the fetus being born handicapped. The alcohol that crosses the placenta barrier remains in the fetus' blood stream and depresses the fetal central nervous system's functioning. Not only does the alcohol disrupt the fetal development, but it is a major source of food energy for the mother. Alcohol contains a great many calories, but is deficient in the nutrients that are needed by a developing fetus. The fetus probably will not receive proper nutrition if the mother indulges in severe alcohol use.

The fetus is often born lighter in weight than it would have if the mother had not been a heavy drinker. Also, the fetus of a heavy drinking mother is born with facial deformities, such as a flat nose and the midline on the upper lip is flattened out and sometimes the fetus has a slanted forehead. These children are irritable as babies and they are always smaller than other children of their age group. They are more likely to be mentally retarded and to be hyperactive to the point of having a learning disability.

AMNIOCENTESIS

In amniocentesis, the physician inserts a needle through the abdominal wall and into the amniotic sac of the pregnant woman and withdraws about one ounce of amniotic fluid from around the fetus. Fetal cells are separated from the fluid and allowed to grow in a culture medium for two to three weeks. The cells are then analyzed for chromosomal abnormalities. Although a variety of genetic disorders can be detected through amniocentesis, it is most often used to detect Down syndrome. In addition, amniocentesis allows one to analyze the amniotic fluid itself. Such analysis can detect about 90 percent of cases of spina bifida, a condition in which the spinal column fails to close during the fetal development. In the fetus with spina bifida, certain proteins leak out of the spinal fluid into the surrounding amniotic sac. The elevation of these proteins enables this defect to be detected. Physicians most often perform amniocentesis at 16 to 18 weeks after the woman's last menstrual period.

CHORIONIC VILLUS SAMPLING

In chorionic villus sampling (CVS), the physician inserts a catheter through the vagina and cervix and withdraws about 1/2000 of an ounce of villi, structures which will later become the placenta. Although first results are often available in two or three days, final verification takes two to three weeks. CVS can detect a variety of chromosomal abnormalities. The major advantage of CVS over amniocentesis is that it can be performed much earlier, between the ninth to eleventh week of pregnancy. If the woman then elects to have an abortion, she can have it with less risk. Some physicians are more hesitant to conduct CVS, however, because, being a newer procedure, less is known about it. In addition, although neither amniocentesis nor CVS is risky, the incidence of miscarriage after CVS is higher than it is after amniocentesis.

SONOGRAPHY

In sonography, high-frequency sound waves or ultrasound are converted into a visual picture of the fetus. This technique can be used to detect some major physical malformations such as spina bifida.

Figure 3.4. Amniocentesis, chorionic villus sampling (CVS), sonography.

Heavy Metals. When we ingest metals such as lead, cadmium, and mercury, the result can be mental retardation or even death. The current attention has been focused on lead, but there is little lead in the atmosphere since we no longer use leaded gasoline. Much of the lead that we do ingest, though, enters the brain and comes from the atmosphere. The use of leaded gasoline has lowered by one-third the blood lead levels in the United States. Also, in recent years, legislation has been passed which has reduced the use of lead in paint and has mandated that leaded paint be removed from the interiors of some older buildings. The leaded paint found in some older homes was at one time a common source of lead poisoning in youngsters. Some children are born with high levels of lead in their blood because the mother to be had been exposed to lead in the atmosphere. The amount of lead in the newborn baby can be determined by an examination of the umbilical cord. On tests of intelligence, the children born with lead in their blood streams scored 8 percent below children who had no levels of lead in their blood. We know that children will place almost anything in their mouths and that includes peeling paint chips. The susceptibility of many children from low socioeconomic backgrounds to lead poisoning may be a combination of poor nutrition and a greater exposure to lead in the older homes in which they live.

PREVENTION

As we learn more and more about the causes of mental retardation, we are in a better position to prevent it. Three levels of prevention have been described: primary, secondary, and tertiary.

Primary prevention focuses on the developing fetus and its objective is to reduce the number of children born mentally retarded. Good prenatal care and teaching pregnant women about the dangers of certain drugs and smoking can prevent some of the cases of mental retardation. Genetic counseling for couples whose children are at risk is another effective way. The effects of rubella have been largely eliminated through antibodies' screening and immunization programs. Scientists will surely discover ways to prevent other diseases causing mental retardation in the future.

Secondary prevention is when we identify and change environmental conditions that could lead to retardation. We already screen newborns for PKU and we can begin treatment and prevent retardation in these newborns. We have eliminated much of the lead in our environment and we are also eliminating other chemicals in our environment.

Tertiary prevention focuses on arranging the educational and social environment so that people who develop mental retardation or are born with mental retardation can achieve their maximum potential and the best quality of life possible for them.

CHARACTERISTICS

The characteristics that distinguish children with mild and moderate retardation from their age-mates are not easily noticed. We find marked differences in factors linked to the intellectual development. Children who have mild retardation act and look just like the rest of society. They are not discovered as retarded until they begin school and later in life they do not have the same job opportunities as other people. One research study found that more than half of the people with mild retardation are unemployed most of the time.

LANGUAGE ACQUISITION AND USE

Children with mental retardation appear to have a general deficit in language development and they also have specific problems using interpretative language. The language of children who are mildly retarded is sparcer in structure and content. These children are also slower in developing in language and the vocabulary they know when they enter school is much less than that of average children.

LEARNING ENVIRONMENTS

In special education, we have what is known as the least restrictive environment principle, which states that a child should be moved from the mainstream of education only as far as necessary to meet his or her educational and social needs. Nevertheless, many children are still educated in the self-contained classroom for the entire day.

RESOURCE ROOM

For children with mild or even moderate retardation, the resource room provides an opportunity to work with special education teachers. The child goes to his or her homeroom first thing in the morning and during the day he or she is sent to the resource room where a special education teacher works with him or her on academic deficiencies. The child can spend no more than one-half of the school day in a resource room and often only spends 45 minutes to an hour there working on specific subjects such as reading, math, spelling, etc.

BEHAVIOR MODIFICATION

Behavior modification is a term which describes a variety of techniques designed to decrease or eliminate obnoxious behavior. It is based on the principles which were developed by B. F. Skinner who found that the systematic application of positive reinforcement after a behavior tended to increase the likelihood that that behavior would not occur again. The educational strategies to arrange the environment so that the behavior that the teacher wants occurs more often than obnoxious behavior. In other words, the teacher should respond positively to the behaviors she wants and should not respond to the unwanted behavior.

Time-out is the physical removal of a child from the classroom for a period of time and is usually done immediately after an unwanted response. Many schools have a period of time-out for one hour, but there are other schools that have a time-out that lasts the entire school day. The child is often asked to return to the resource room or the self-contained classroom when he or she feels that unacceptable behavior will not occur again.

Contingent social reinforcement is the token system. A token is given to the child and when he or she has acted appropriately, the token can be used to buy things. The tokens are saved and cashed in for toys or time to do a puzzle or play a game. In some schools, the tokens can be cashed in for certain types of candy or fruit that are considered appropriate for good health.

The use of behavior modification techniques with the mildly handicapped has helped increase academic response rates and also attendance of handicapped children. The use of behavior modification has also helped achievement in grades and has encouraged verbal interchange between the teacher and the child and the teacher and the child's parents.

REFERENCES

Capron, C., & Duyme, M. (1989, August 17). Assessment of socio-economic status on IQ in a full cross-fostering study. *Nature, 552–553.*

Grossman, H. (Ed.). (1983). *Manual on terminology and classification in mental retardation.* Washington, DC: American Association on Mental Deficiency.

Heber, R. F. (1961). A manual on terminology and classification in mental retardation (rev. ed.). Monograph Supplement, *American Journal of Mental Deficiency, 64.*

Kirk, S., Gallagher, J., & Anastasiow, N. (1993). *Educating exceptional children* (7th ed.). Boston: Houghton Mifflin.

MacMillan, D. L. (1982). *Mental retardation in school and society (2nd ed.).* Boston: Little, Brown.

Skeels, H., & Dye, H. (1939). A study of the effects of differential stimulation on mentally retarded children. *Proceedings of the American Association on Mental Deficiency,* *44,* 114–136.

U.S. Department of Education. (1989). *Tenth annual report to Congress on the implemen-* *tation of the Education of the Handicapped Act.* Washington, DC: U.S. Department of Education.

U.S. Department of Education. (1991). To assure free appropriate public education of all handicapped children. *Thirteenth annual report to Congress on the implementation of* *the Education of the Handicapped Act.* Washington, DC: U.S. Government Printing Office.

Wesling, D. (1986). *Introduction to mental retardation.* Englewood Cliffs, NJ: Prentice-Hall.

Chapter 4

LEARNING DISABILITIES

No other area in special education has generated such controversy as learning disabilities. We are intrigued by learning disabilities because children with LD have an average or higher intelligence quotient (IQ) but do not succeed in learning to read and write. They do not possess mental retardation, mental disturbances, visual or hearing impairments, or environmental deprivations. Researchers tell us that there is no one cause of the difficulties experienced by people who are said to have learning disabilities. There appear to be many causes and not all children with LD have the same problems. Most, however, have trouble learning to read and write. For example, 85 percent have trouble learning to read. There is a high correlation between learning to read and learning to write. Some have trouble with math. The majority who have trouble with reading also have trouble with math.

A BRIEF HISTORY OF LEARNING DISABILITIES

For a long time we have been intrigued with the child with average intelligence but who does not succeed in school. Researchers began investigating the causes of this disability in the 1800s and we still investigate this anomaly today. Although many questions remain, poor teaching and poor effort on the part of the child have been ruled out.

Alfred Strauss was a German neurologist who became prominent during the 1940s. He began the groundwork for the field of learning disabilities that we know today.

Strauss observed brain-injured students and noticed that they had common patterns of behavior. He would later come to America and do similar work. He became interested in children who were excluded from public schools due to mental retardation, cerebral palsy, hyperactivity, or other problems. He observed that the public schools either could not or would not adapt to the children's needs. Strauss also observed that these students had common patterns of behaviors that matched the behaviors of the brain-injured soldiers he had worked with in Germany. He established the Cove School for the purpose of educating brain-injured children, and to further research the disorder.

Because the term "brain-injured" was confusing, in that all children with brain injuries have learning disorders, and because it was difficult to use this term in communicating with parents, many other terms were suggested for describing these children. For example, Strauss Syndrome, Minimal Brain Dysfunction, and Learning Disabled.

This history is important because it provided the fundamentals and laid the foundation for the later efforts of Cruickshank, Kirk, and Myklebust. It was the beginning of the field of learning disabilities. This foundation was basically imbedded in three ways. First, Strauss and his associates perceived a homogeneity in a diverse group of children who had been misdiagnosed by specialists, misunderstood by parents, and discarded by society. Second, they planned and implemented educational settings and procedures to teach such children successfully. Third, they alerted many professions to the existence of a new category of exceptional children.

The criterion by which Strauss identified and diagnosed brain-injured children are as follows:

1. History—is there evidence of injury before, during, or after birth?
2. Slight neurological signs present indicate brain lesions.
3. When disturbances are so severe that measurable retardation is observable, and history indicates that the child comes from a normal family, and is the only sibling affected.
4. When no mental retardation exists, presence of psychological disturbance can be discovered by the use of Strauss' qualitative test for perceptual and conceptual disturbances.

Over the years, a number of hypotheses were proposed to explain the disorder. Orton (1937), a neurologist at the University of Iowa, believed that the difficulty stemmed from the failure of the left hemisphere of the brain to take on the role of language, as is typical in other human beings. He called this "twisted symbols," which caused children to reverse letters such as *pot* for *top* or *gas* for *sag*. Orton also referred to these children as "brain damaged." Later, Clements and Peters (1962) would refer to these children as minimally brain damaged. Kirk and Kirk (1971) and Myklebust (1968) perceived the problems in terms of specific language disorder. Fernald (1943) and Gillingham and Stillman (1960) thought the disorder was directly related to the area of written language.

Samuel Kirk (1966), at a meeting of concerned parents, proposed the term learning disabilities and it was greeted warmly by the parents. The term was widely adopted and is still used today.

Today, most of the theories about brain damage being the cause of learning disabilities have been abandoned or revised; however, the causes of the disorder are generally unknown.

Educators, researchers, and parents are supported by organizations such as the Council for Exceptional Children (whose learning disabilities division was founded in 1972), the Orton Society, and the American Committee on Learning Disabilities (ACLD), which is now known as the Learning Disabilities Association (LDA). These groups encouraged legislation such as the Specific Learning Disabilities Act of 1969 (Public Law 91–230) and the Individual with Disabilities Education Act (IDEA) of 1990.

Definitions

We know that children with learning disabilities perceive the world in a way that is different from most of us. The following are some of the most accepted definitions:

The Federal Register (1977) includes the regulations for identifying and defining students with learning disabilities under Public Law 94–142 (PL94–142):

> "Specific learning disability" means a disorder in one or more of basic psychological processes involved in using language, spoken or written, which may manifest itself in an imperfect ability to listen, think, speak, read, write, spell, or to do mathematical calculations. The term includes such conditions as perceptual handicaps, brain injury, minimal brain dysfunction, dyslexia, and developmental aphasia. The term does not include children who have learning problems which are primarily the result of visual, hearing, or motor handicaps, of mental retardation, of emotional disturbance, or of environmental, cultural, or economic disadvantage. (USOE, 1977, p. 650)

The Federal Register definition has four criteria that must be considered when identifying students with learning disabilities.

1. *Academic difficulties.* The child with learning disabilities has difficulty learning how to read or do mathematical calculations, compared with other children of the same age.

2. *Discrepancy between potential and achievement.* The child with learning disabilities experiences a serious discrepancy between intellectual ability and school achievement; this is known as an **aptitude-achievement discrepancy.**
3. *Exclusion of other factors.* A person may not be classified as having learning disabilities if the learning problem is caused by visual or hearing impairment, mental retardation, motor disabilities, emotional disturbance, or environmental factors.
4. *Neurological disorder.* Basic learning disabilities are the result of some type of neurological disorder.

Summarizing the criteria in PL 94–142, one can say that the field can be divided into two distinct areas of activity: (1) those who seek the source of the difficulty and (2) those who try to design curricula and teaching strategies to enable persons with learning disabilities to learn academic subjects in spite of the source of their difficulties.

The definition has been modified over time, but the National Joint Committee for Learning Disabilities (1991) proposed the following:

Learning disabilities is a generic term that refers to a heterogeneous group of disorders that are manifested by significant difficulties in the acquisition and use of listening, speaking, reading, writing, reasoning, or mathematical abilities. These disorders are intrinsic to the individual and are presumed to be due to central nervous system dysfunction. Even though a learning disability may occur concomitantly with other handicapping conditions (e.g., sensory impairment, mental retardation, social and emotional disturbances, insufficient/inappropriate instruction, psychogenic factors), it is not the result of those conditions or influences (p. 16).

The use of the term *central nervous system dysfunction* means that the definition assumes that the brain, perceptual systems, or both are not damaged but work in a way that is different from those of children without learning problems. Learning disabilities are suspected to arise out of differences in brain and perceptual functioning rather than from specific damage to those systems.

Both definitions point to the need to present an alternative set of lessons to match the unusual neurological patterns these children possess. Much of the special education designed for these children focuses on strategies to help the student master lessons they could not learn from the traditional curriculum.

It is important to bear in mind the following:

- All children with learning disabilities have learning problems.
- Not all children with academic problems have learning disabilities.

Therefore, one cannot say that children with Down's syndrome have learning disabilities. They may need special help because of their lower cognitive abilities caused by the disorder. Other children may have trouble learning in academic settings because of the disorganized environment in which they live or emotional trauma they have experienced. These children are not considered by definition to have learning disabilities.

At this time, the following is known:

1. *Learning disabilities* is a general term referring to a heterogeneous group of disorders that includes different subgroups.
2. Learning disabilities must be viewed as a problem not only of the school years but also of early childhood and adult life.
3. A learning disability is intrinsic to the individual with the basis of the disorder presumed to be central nervous system dysfunction.
4. Learning disabilities may occur with other handicapping conditions as well as within cultural and linguistic groups (Kavale, Forness & Bender, 1987, Vol. 1, p. 6).

Satz, Morrison, and Fletcher (1985) summarized a host of hypotheses as to the cause of learning disabilities. They conclude that there are many types of children with learning disabilities and while the deficits may have been identified, their cause or causes are still widely unknown.

The deficits that exist in the brain are referred to as developmental learning disabilities. Identified or hypothesized subgroups include deficits in the following areas:

- Nonverbal communication
- Learning Strategies
- Short-term memory
- Maturational pace (hence, a lag in development)
- Processing verbal information
- Perceptual process—auditory or visual
- Neurological structures
- Motivation
- Genes or generic disorders (Satz, Morrison & Fletcher, 1985)

Prevalence

The Interagency Committee (1990) concluded that 4 percent of the children in school have been classified as having learning disabilities (p. 139). Forty percent of the children are in special education programs while the rest are in the regular classroom.

Kirk, Gallagher and Anastasiow (1993) report the following:

The distribution in the United States is not geographic and varies from state to state. For example, Rhode Island reported that 63 percent of the special education population in the state has learning disabilities; Alabama reported only 26 percent of its population."

The problem with prevalence figures lies in the lack of uniform definitions of learning disabilities across the states and a failure to administer a complex multidisciplinary assessment that encompasses social, genetic, cultural, and educational factors. As there is no single cause for school failure, some factors have to be ruled out (such as severe hearing impairments or cultural deprivation) before a child is considered as having learning disabilities (Interagency Committee, 1990, p. 140). Currently, the category of learning disabilities contains the largest number of students in special education (Kavale, Forness & Bender, Vol. 1, 1987). Some schools tend to identify all students in academic trouble as having learning disabilities, and this causes the number of children so identified to change dramatically.

We have a large number of children in our schools who fall into the IQ range of 70–90. According to the WISC–III (1991), they make up 23.5 percent. Wechsler (1991) refers to them as low average; other educators and psychologists refer to them as slow learners. This is a large group of children and they gradually fall further and further behind their age group in academics. For example, a child in the sixth grade who has an IQ of 80 will function about two to three years behind his peers in academics. This child does not have learning disabilities because he does not have a severe discrepancy between potential and achievement. If we look closely at the children throughout America who have been identified as LD, we will find a large number of them to be slow learners who do not have a learning disability.

Characteristics

Imagine being a sixth grade teacher in the 1950s and you have in your classroom a child (probably a boy) who reads at the middle second grade level, works arithmetic at the beginning third grade level, and the completion of academic tasks involving language are impossible. School psychologists were scarce in the 1950s, but let's say your school system employed one. The school psychologist finds the boy has high average intelligence. You meet with the parents who are just as baffled as you.

You find out that the child was perfectly happy before he entered school and nobody suspected that anything was wrong. The little boy was slightly hyperactive and did not always pay attention to the full story or even listen to the whole sentence. Once in school and problems in academics were encountered, the boy began having behavior problems. In those days we found all kinds of reasons for his behavior and failure:

lazy, immature, sorry, parents are at fault, poor teachers, no discipline at home, etc. The list was endless.

Schumaker, Deshler, and McNight (1991), in a year long study of the characteristics of adolescents with learning disabilities, found the following:

- The adolescents with learning disabilities they studied had reached a plateau and were making little progress in academic skills. The tenth-grade students were reading and doing arithmetic at fifth- and sixth-grade levels.
- The adolescents with learning disabilities showed deficiencies in study skills. They were less efficient than other students in note taking, listening comprehension, monitoring writing errors, test taking, and scanning.
- Many of the adolescents showed immature problem-solving skills. They were unable to create and apply strategies to new problems.

Deshler and Schumaker (1983) came to the conclusion that most adolescents with LD have social skill deficiencies as well as younger children who suffer from LD.

Kavale, Forness, and Bender (1988) state that a large number of researchers are focusing on how to solve academic learning problems by developing teaching strategies and curriculum. Figure 4.1 shows the academic problem areas that teachers are most concerned with and they want to focus on this academic perspective in solving the academic problems of LD children.

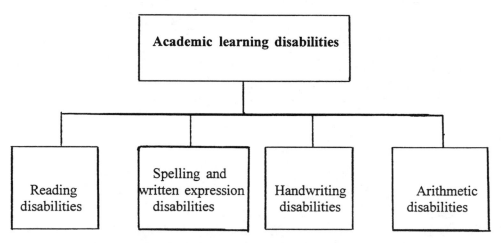

Figure 4.1. Academic learning disabilities.

Other researchers want to focus on what they call developmental learning disabilities. A developmental perspective on learning disabilities involves seeking an underlying cause for students' difficulties in academic subjects. Figure 4.2 points out the developmental areas and a large number of researchers are pursuing the source or cause of these disorders (Kavale, Forness & Bender, 1987, 1988).

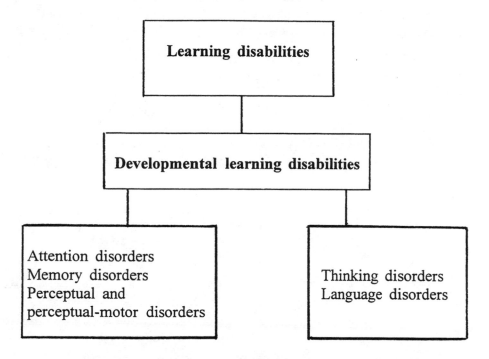

Figure 4.2. Learning disabilities.

Hardman, Drew et al. tell us that educational services for children with LD were virtually nonexistent prior to the 1960s. They further state that learning disabilities have generated more controversy, confusion, and polarization among contemporary professionals than any other exceptionality.

In years past, many students now identified as having specific learning disabilities would have been labeled *remedial readers, remedial learners, emotionally handicapped,* or *mentally retarded* — if they received any special help or additional instructional support at all. Today, learning disabilities command the largest single program for exceptional children in the United States. It is relatively new, but its growth rate has been unparalleled by any other area in special education (U.S. Department of Education, 1991).

Kirk, Gallagher, and Anastasiow (1993) imply and state that for a child to have LD he must have average or above intelligence: "Children who have normal intelligence and no classifiable disability yet who do not succeed in school have been a concern to teachers, parents, researchers, and the children themselves" (p. 223). The aforementioned three (1993) also state, "They are not able to do what others with the same level of intelligence are able to do" (p. 223).

This author believes strongly that we are classifying children as having LD without comparing their functioning with their ability and the ability of other children with the same level of intelligence. This large group of slow learners can have LD, but most of them don't.

Learning Disabilities and ADD

A condition that is often associated with LD that is not defined in the Individuals with Disabilities Education Act (IDEA) of 1990 (PL 101–476) is attention-deficit disorder (ADD). We know that many children with LD have ADD, but probably less than half. The primary problem a child with ADD has is the inability to concentrate for a long period of time. Attention-deficit disorders, as we currently conceive it, actually include two subcategories, attention-deficit hyperactivity disorder (ADHD) and undifferentiated attention-deficit disorder (UADD) (APA, 1987). The primary characteristics of both conditions is a child's inability to concentrate for a long period of time (Hardman, Drew et al., 1993). ADD is defined as a disorder in children who have difficulties maintaining an attention span because of their limited ability to concentrate and who exhibit impulsive actions (Lahey, Schaughency et al., 1987). The two sub-categories—ADHD and UADD—as defined in the *Diagnostic and Statistical Manual of Mental Disorders* (3rd ed. rev.) (DSM III–R), were developed to distinguish between children who exhibited hyperactive behavior and those who did not (APA, 1987).

Hardman, Drew et al. state:

> Individuals with either of the ADD diagnoses will have attention-span problems, being generally unable to focus on a specific task for a sustained period. They will also evidence impulsiveness and often commit actions with no apparent fore-thought of what is involved or what the consequences might be. For children who are diagnosed as ADHD, the characteristic of excessive motor activity (especially in inappropriate situations) will be evident. These youngsters are thus seen as being hyperactive, a characteristic long identified with some children who have learning disabilities. Those children who are not hyperactive but exhibit attention or concentration difficulties should be diagnosed as UADD. (Hardman, Drew et al., 1993)

Prevalence estimates for ADD suggest that about 3 percent of all children may have the disorder (APA, 1987). Research indicates that males with ADD outnumber females in ratios from 2:1 to 10:1 (McGee, Williams & Silva, 1987).

Aleman (1990) tells us that children with ADD do not qualify under IDEA unless they also have another disability condition that is defined in the law. In IDEA, ADD was viewed as a characteristic of a learning disability but not as a disabling condition by itself. Hardman, Drew et al. (1993) report that the use of ADD terminology had begun growing during the 1980s and this expanded use, plus the DSM–III–R (APA, 1987), have prompted consideration of including ADD in federal legislation.

Identification and Assessment of LD

Kirk, Gallagher, and Anastasiow (1993) tell us that identifying children with learning disabilities is not easy. "First, learning disabilities must be distinguished from other conditions, and then the difference between potential and achievement must be evaluated. How large a discrepancy should there be? Must a child have an identifiable developmental learning disability that has contributed to educational underachievement? Who makes the decision?" (p. 238).

School systems under the provisions of IDEA are required to assemble a multidisciplinary team of professionals to examine the child psychologically, mentally, socially, and educationally, and, with the parents, come to a decision on whether the child is eligible for special education. The identification process followed by most school systems includes these steps.

1. A teacher or parent refers the child for evaluation.
2. The referral is evaluated by a committee of teachers, including the special education teacher, to determine whether the child should be assessed by a multidisciplinary team.
3. Once an assessment is approved, parental permission for the assessment is obtained.
4. The evaluation is conducted by a multidisciplinary team including psychologists, social workers, the classroom teacher, and the special education teacher.
5. Team members hold a conference and decide whether the child is eligible for special education.

6. If the child is eligible, an individualized education program (IEP) is formulated and the child is placed in the appropriate service.

Many are concerned today about the number of children enrolled in special education programs for learning disabilities and other handicapping conditions. To reduce the possibility that children who actually do not need special programs will be identified as those who do, many schools have implemented a prereferral process, in which a teacher-assistance team (of classroom teachers with or without special education teachers) meets to discuss children who appear to have learning problems. Chalfant (1985) described the functions of the team:

- Clarifying "the nature of learning and behavior problems"
- Generating "instructional alternatives for the classroom"
- Monitoring "the implementation of recommendations"
- Referring "students for individual testing" (p. 15)

As a rule, classroom teachers attempt to cope with learning problems before referring a child for special education. For some children with mild or even moderate learning problems, prereferral adaptations are sufficient and special education programs are not needed.

Guidelines for the Assessment of Learning Disabilities

Barkley (1981) tells us that in the assessment of learning-disabled children, it is important to evaluate the following:

- *developmental-cognitive processes* (for example, verbal-linguistic, visual-spatial-constructional, sequential-analytic, and planning processes);
- *achievement skills* (for example, reading, spelling, mathematics, and written expression);
- *environmental demands* (for example, demands on the child in the school and family);
- *reactions of others* (for example, how the parents, teachers, and peers respond to the child's failures); and
- *interaction effects* (for example, how the above areas interact over time to affect the child's performance and adjustment).

Assessment Questions

Useful questions related to assessment of the above-mentioned factors include the following (Barkley, 1981c, pp. 461–462).

1. What are the nature and the extent of deficits in those cognitive skills that are important to academic achievement? What is the nature of the errors in performance?

2. Can the origin of the learning disability be determined?
3. With what particular tasks in the classroom are the cognitive deficits interfering (such as mathematics, reading, or spelling)?
4. What are the nature and the extent of primary or secondary emotional behaviors that may occur with, or be a reaction to, the learning disability?
5. How are the learning disability and its concomitant behavioral-emotional disorders affecting the child's interactions with and reactions from parents, teachers, and peers? In what setting are these interactional problems most likely to occur?
6. How will the factors at these various levels of analysis interact over time to improve or exacerbate the child's problems?
7. How can the child's remaining cognitive "strengths" be used in habilitating or coping with the existing problems?
8. What resources exist within the family, school, and community that can be used to assist in habilitation.

Assessment Battery

According to Sattler (1988), the most important tools in the assessment of learning-disabled children are reliable and valid intelligence and achievement tests that assess major content areas such as reading, mathematics, and spelling. Although there is no one standard battery for the assessment of learning disability, many tests are useful. As always, the selection of tests should be based partly on the referral questions. Evaluating auditory skills and visual/perceptual processing skills, in addition to intelligence and achievement skills, may be helpful. Ideally, diagnostic procedures should not be conducted outside of the classroom; rather, they should be an ongoing part of the regular classroom activity—particularly after the psychoeducational evaluation and related studies have been completed.

The assessment of reading-disabled children should focus on the child's skills in reading—such as repertoire of words identified on sight; knowledge of speech sounds, such as vowels, consonants, and blends; comprehension skills; silent reading skills; and oral reading skills—and should incorporate trial remediation procedures.

Learning Disabilities and the WISC–III

Attempts have been made to determine whether various WISC–IIIs (or WISC–R) patterns, such as verbal-performance discrepancy, pattern of subtest scores, and range of subtest scores can distinguish learning disabled children from normal children, problem behavior children, and mentally retarded children. Bannatyne (1974) proposed that the WISC subtests be recategorized as follows to aid in evaluating learning disabled children:

> Spatial: Picture Completion, Block Design, and Object Assembly.
> Conceptual: Comprehension, Similarities, and Vocabulary.
> Sequential: Arithmetic, Digit Span, and Coding.
> Acquired Knowledge: Information, Arithmetic, and Vocabulary.

Sattler (1988) goes on to explain this in the following way:

> The spatial categories samples the ability to manipulate objects in multidimensional space, either directly or symbolically. The conceptual category covers abilities related to language development. The sequential category is the same as the freedom from distractibility factor found in WISC–III factor analytic studies; it reflects the ability to retain and use sequences of auditory and memory stimuli in short term memory stories. The acquired knowledge category represents abilities usually learned in school or at home.

Bannatyne's (1974) recategorization was based on an inspection of the subtests, not on factor analytic findings. It is simply a holistic model designed to aid in test interpretation. The pattern proposed to be characteristic of learning disabilities is spacial equals conceptual equals sequential.

Sattler (1988) states: "Unfortunately, attempts to find unique WISC–R patterns among learning disabled children have not been successful. After an extensive investigation of 94 WISC–R studies with learning disabled children, Kavale and Forness (1984) reported that no recategorization of WISC–R scores, profiles, factor clusters, or patterns revealed a significant difference between the learning disabled and normal samples. Even within the learning disabled group, no regrouping scheme was found to be useful in differential diagnosis" (pp. 609, 610).

Miller, Stoneburger, and Brecht (1978) said that the failure to find unique WISC–R patterns for learning disabled children is not surprising. Learning disabled children represent a group that is too heterogeneous for one type WISC–R profile to be typical of all or even most of its members. Thus, for example, the Bannatyne reorganizations have not been successful in differentiating children with visual-perceptual deficits from those with auditory-perceptual deficits. Furthermore, it has not been a successful venture to differentiate learning disabled children from (a) normal children with average intelligence, (b) emotionally disturbed or mentally retarded children, or slow learners, or other types of exceptional children.

Sattler (1988) states that these results strongly suggest that a child's

WISC–R profile should not be used to establish a diagnosis of learning disabilities.

There has been very little research done to date on the WISC–III profiles and the establishment of learning disabilities. However, in all of the research quoted, and there are at least 100 studies which indicate that there is no pattern of WISC or WISC–R subtest scores to differentiate learning disabled children from other children, we can assume that there are no WISC–III profiles which will differentiate LD children from other types of children.

Defining a Severe Discrepancy

The indicator most frequently used to identify learning disability in children is an ability-achievement discrepancy. Children who are low achievers in school, yet of average or above intelligence, are candidates for identification based on this criterion. The major classification problem centers on how to define a severe discrepancy between *ability,* usually defined by an intelligence test score, and *achievement,* usually defined by a reading, arithmetic, or spelling test score or by an overall achievement score (Sattler, 1988).

1. Deviation from grade or age level. Underachievement is most simply defined as a discrepancy between the child's grade-equivalent score on an achievement test and his or her grade placement. For example, a sixth-grade child who obtains a grade-equivalent score that is at the third-grade level would be characterized as being three years below grade placement. Some definitions use a graduated deviation criterion in which the amount of deviation required between grade placement and achievement varies as a function of current grade placement. The discrepancy may be one year in first and second grades, one and a half years in third and fourth grades, two years in fifth through eighth grades, and three years in ninth through twelfth grades.

2. Expectancy formulas. Expected grade equivalent, rather than actual grade-placement, may be used in the computation of an ability-achievement discrepancy. Expectancy formulas are based on the child's mental age (MA) and chronological age (CA). Examples of expectancy formulas follow:

The Mental Grade Method (Harris, 1961)

This is the simplest method. To estimate reading expectancy, five is subtracted from the mental age.

RE (reading expectance) = MA (mental age) − 5

Jimmy is 10-0 and has a mental age of 12-0. His reading expectancy is therefore grade 7.

9 (RE) = 12 (MA) − 5

If Jimmy reads at the 3.0 grade level, he has a four-year discrepancy in reading.

Years-in-School Method (Bond & Tinker, 1967, pp. 198–203)

This method takes into account the school exposure the child has had.

$$RE \text{ (reading expectancy)} = \frac{\text{years in school} \times IQ}{100} + 1.0$$

Ten-year-old Jimmy is in the middle of fifth grade, that is, he has been in school for 4.5 years. His IQ score is 120. Using this formula, we find that his reading expectancy grade is 6.4.

$$RE = \frac{4.5 \times 120}{100} + 1.0 = 6.4$$

Since Jimmy reads at the 3.0 grade level, the discrepancy between expectancy and achievement levels is 3.4 years.

Learning Quotient Method (Myklebust, 1968)

This method determines discrepancy in terms of a quotient, that is, what percentage of his or her ability to learn has the child fulfilled? There are two steps in this method:

$$(1)\ EA \text{ (expectancy age)} = \frac{MA + CA + GA \text{ (grade age)}}{3}$$

$$(2)\ LQ \text{ (learning quotient)} = \frac{AA \text{ (achievement age)}}{EA \text{ (expectancy age)}}$$

Note that in this method, all scores are converted from grade scores to age scores (grade score + 5 = age score). What is Jimmy's learning quotient with this method?

$$(1)\ EA = \frac{12.0 + 10.0 + 10.5}{3}$$

$$(2)\ LD = \frac{8.0}{10.8} = 7.4$$

Early Intervention

It is obvious that the earlier we identify children with learning disabilities, the sooner we can begin intervention programs that will help them. More importantly, if we can identify children who are at risk for learning disabilities, we may be able to prevent those disabilities.

Badian (1982, 1988), in a longitudinal study in which she tried to determine if preschoolers could be screened to identify those at risk for learning disabilities, looked at tests that screened for possible reading problems. She followed a group of preschoolers, testing them before they began school at age four, in the third grade, and again in the eighth grade. She found that two tests, the Information and Sentences subtests of the Wechsler Preschool and Primary Scale of Intelligence, predicted with a fairly high degree of accuracy the long-term performance of the students in reading. The Information subtest assesses factual knowledge and the Sentences subtest assesses the ability to repeat increasingly complex sentences. Moreover, she found that certain characteristics such as a troubled birth history, family history of learning disabilities, a late order of birth among siblings, delayed speech development, and lower socioeconomic status differentiated poor readers from good readers. If we can identify learning disabilities in preschool children, then later on we can do the educational things which will keep these children from being learning disabled when they reach junior high or high school. We must observe behavior of children and compare their behavior with age appropriate tasks. These tasks often involve preacademic readiness skills such as cutting with scissors, holding a crayon, sharing an experience with a classmate, or even drawing a crude picture of a person. Some children have trouble with fine and gross motor development. Other children are slow to develop oral language and reasoning abilities. These delays in information processes can affect a child's learning, his ability to communicate, and his social and emotional adjustment. The most common disorders among preschoolers are delayed language development, poor perceptual-motor skills, and lack of attention.

When we diagnose preschool children, the examiners rely on observations by parents and teachers, and by rating scales, informal clinical diagnoses, and norm-referenced and criterion-referenced tests. We function very much like detectives when we gather these clues and we formulate and discard hypotheses until we arrive at the solution that we hope best fits the available evidence.

Language Disabilities

The most common learning disabilities which we note at the preschool level are language disabilities. According to Kirk, Gallagher, and Anastasiow (1993), in order to diagnose a disability, the psychoeducational examiner should follow a series of steps:

1. Obtain a description of the language behavior as observed by the parents, the preschool teacher, or both.
2. Review the medical record to see whether the disability can be explained medically.
3. Study the family situation to determine whether factors in the home contribute to the disability.
4. Using formal and informal tests, examine the child's abilities and disabilities in understanding language, relating things heard to past experiences, and talking.
5. Determine what the child can and cannot do in a specific area. For example, if the child functions well in most areas but does not talk, the next step is to find out if he or she understands language. If the child does not understand oral language, the next step is to find out if he or she can discriminate among words, among phonemes, or among common sounds in the environment.
6. Organize a remedial program that moves the child step by step into areas in which the child could not initially perform. (pp. 241, 242)

Perceptual-Motor Disabilities

Children with perceptual-motor disabilities have trouble understanding and responding to the meaning of pictures or numbers. When we diagnose perceptual-motor disabilities in preschoolers, psychoeducational examiners ask the usual questions about medical and home background and through ratings, interviews, and formal tests try to discover the contributing factors and areas in which the child experiences major difficulties. In the process, examiners try to answer several questions:

1. Can the child interpret the environment and the significance of what he or she sees?
2. Can the child match shapes and colors?
3. Can the child recognize visual objects and pictures rapidly?
4. Can the child assemble puzzles?
5. Can the child express ideas in motor (nonverbal) terms through gestures and drawings? (Kirk, Gallagher, and Anastasiow, 1993)

Memory Problems

Memory is crucial to the learning process, and it is well documented that children with learning disabilities have difficulty remembering academic and content matter such as math facts, words, rules, etc. Many authorities recognize that there are several types of memory: short-term memory, long-term memory, sequential memory, rote memory, recall, and recognition. Hallahan and Kauffman (1988) note that students with learning disabilities usually have problems remembering auditory and visual stimuli. Swanson, Cochran, and Ewers (1990) found that measures of memory differentiate students with learning disabilities from slow learners, average students, and above average students. These authors note that students with learning disabilities exhibit distinct deficiencies in working memory. Teachers frequently report that students with learning disabilities forget spelling words, math facts, and directions. Torgesen and Kail (1980) provide the following conclusions:

1. Students with learning disabilities fail to use strategies that students without disabilities readily use. For example, in learning a list of words, students without disabilities will rehearse the names to themselves or group the words in categories for studying. Generally, students with learning disabilities do not use these strategies spontaneously.
2. Students with learning disabilities may have difficulty remembering because of their poor language skills. Thus, verbal material may be particularly difficult to remember. (p. 133)

ACADEMIC LEARNING DISABILITIES

It has been written by many authors that academic learning disabilities include deficits in reading, writing, spelling, and mathematics. Kirk, Gallagher, and Anastasiow (1993) state, "how to teach these subjects to students with learning disabilities has been the subject of a long debate; no general consensus exists as to which model is best" (p. 230).

Reading Disorders

Several months after birth, children start using auditory skills to match objects with names. It stands to reason, then, that auditory discrimination is the first sense used in learning to read. When a child obtains a mental age between 6.0 and 6.6 (years and months), he will begin matching his own auditory sound system to an abstract system of print. In English, we have 26 letters of the alphabet which are abstract symbols of a sound system which consists of consonants and vowels. The vowels (a, e, i, o, u, and sometimes y) combine with the other letters (consonants) to make up 48 phonemes which are the smallest units of sound meaning.

Authorities believe that language is developed in different ways, and because reading is a part of language, it makes sense that reading is developed differently by children also. The following theories are often mentioned:

1. Behaviorists believe that language is developed through training (stimulus, response, and reinforcement).
2. Piaget theorists explain language in terms of stages at different periods.
3. Biological theorists believe that language is developed by an inherently determined set of factors.

This author believes children use the following methods of processing when learning to read and in the order presented.

1. Auditory and auditory association
2. Auditory memory
3. Auditory blending
4. Visual discrimination
5. Visual memory
6. Visual blending

The following problems could very well prevent a child with learning disabilities from learning to read:

1. Faulty auditory perception without hearing impairment
2. Slow auditory and visual processing
3. Inability to perceive words (dyslexia)
4. Lack of knowledge and purpose of reading
5. Failure to attend to critical aspects of the word, sentence, or paragraph
6. Failure to understand that units of speech are represented by letters (Clark, 1988; Liberman & Liberman, 1990; Curtis & Tallal, 1991; Goodman, 1976)

Dyslexia

Ekwall and Shauker (1988) cite that one of the first reports of a child with dyslexia to appear in the literature was written by a British physician, Pringle Morgan (1896). In his report Morgan wrote:

Percy F.—a well-grown lad, aged 14 . . . is the eldest son of intelligent parents, the second child in a family of seven. He has always been a bright and intelligent boy, quick at games and in no way inferior to others of his age. His greatest difficulty . . . his inability to learn to read . . . is remarkable, and is pronounced, and I have no doubt it is due to some congenital defect. He has been at school or under tutors since he was seven years old, and the greatest efforts have been made to teach him to read, but in spite of this laborious and persistent training, he can only with difficulty spell words of one syllable. . . . The schoolmaster who has taught him for some years says that he would be the smartest lad in the school if the instruction were purely oral . . .

Many teachers recognize this boy. This type child has always been in the classrooms.

The reader may have guessed by now that dyslexia is the name we give to a condition that causes a severe reading disorder. Currently, dyslexia is considered a subgroup disorder within the learning disabilities category. Rourke (1991) explains that children with dyslexia have a variety of deficits resulting from brain dysfunction. The brain is not damaged, but it operates differently from the brain of a child who does not have dyslexia. The layman might say that this child has a loose wire in the brain or a "short" in the wiring system.

An ophthalmologist, J. A. Fisher (1910), was an early teacher of reading and felt that these disabilities were due to structural damage to the brain. As already discussed, Samuel Orton, in the 1930s, developed a comprehensive theory of learning disabilities based on the neurological model. He coined the word *strephosymbolia* which means "twisted symbols." He further postulated that the brain does not develop a dominant side and, therefore, the child suffers from mixed dominance. Orton believed that this abnormality of the brain's development was genetically determined because he noticed that it tended to "run in families."

Most of Orton's theories have not fared well with the passing of time, but as a pediatrician, Melvin Levine (1980), said, "Orton's pioneering work encouraged further research."

Dyslexia was one of the earliest labels used along with "word blindness" to define a child like the one described by Dr. Morgan in 1896.

Techniques for Remediation of Dyslexia. The following techniques are good for the child suffering from dyslexia. Love & Litton (1994) write about the Fernald Approach and the Orton Gillingham Method.

Fernald Approach

Grace Fernald, a psychologist, developed her method of teaching children to read in an attempt to enable children with "word blindness" to learn to read. Her approach was used in a one-to-one situation with children that had failed to learn to read in conventional settings.

The children in her classroom made up their own stories, dictating them to their teachers, rather than using a reader. The child then learned to read and spell the words used in his story. Words were written in cursive because the child learned the word as a total pattern, tracing the entire word, and thereby strengthening his memory and visualization of the entire word.

The Fernald Approach is a multisensory method of teaching reading, writing, and spelling. The following steps are involved:

1. The child is told he is going to learn words in a new way that has proved to be very successful. The words in the story he has dictated are presented to him one at a time.
2. The teacher writes the word on a piece of paper, 4 inches by 10 inches, as the child watches and as the teacher says the word.
3. The child traces the word with one or two fingers, saying it several times. When he feels that he has mastered the spelling of the word, he writes it with his finger on the table. The next step is to write the word on a separate piece of paper while saying it.
4. The word is then written from memory without looking at the original copy. If it is incorrect, the tracing and saying steps are repeated. If the word is correct, it is put in a file box. The words in the file box are used in later stories.
5. At later stages this painstaking tracing method for learning words is not needed. Now the child learns a word by **looking** as the teacher writes it, **saying** it, and **writing** it. At a still later stage, the child can learn by only looking at a word in print and writing it, and, finally by merely looking at it.

The Orton-Gillingham Method

The Orton-Gillingham remediation technique is an alphabetic phonic approach to teaching language skills using the multi-sensory method of eyes (visual), ears (auditory), and muscles (kinesthetic). This is an alphabetic method which concentrates on fusing smaller units into more complex wholes. This method is for students who have been unable to acquire reading, writing, and spelling skills using traditional methods. It has been found to be effective with students who have specific types of reading disabilities.

This method was developed by Anna Gillingham and Bessie Stillman in the 1930s as an instructional treatment for the kinds of children diagnosed by Samuel Orton as language-disordered. Orton's theory stated that reading problems occurred in these children because of an incomplete cerebral hemispheric dominance. When Samuel Orton died, a group of his associates formed the Orton Society to continue his work. Today, the Orton Society is a nonprofit, scientific and educational organization.

This method emphasizes drill and repetition. It requires exclusiveness. No other method of teaching should be used if you are using this method. The authors require that the remedial lessons be held daily for a minimum of two years to be effective. This method was also designed for children identified as dyslexic, described as having normal or superior intelligence but unable to acquire reading skills by ordinary school methods.

The materials included in this method are: a 344-page, hardcover manual describing in detail this method of teaching, each phonic unit is presented on separate Drill Cards, twenty Word Cards with familiar words which can be made from the first ten letters introduced in the drill cards, and graded phonetic stories, exercises on syllable division and practice in the use of a dictionary are additional methods in this remedial approach.

This method has several criticisms. It does not make an accommodation for children with auditory discrimination and auditory perception problems. The procedures are overly rigid, the reading material in this program is not interesting, and the reading of other methods is delayed. Children instructed in this approach have a tendency to develop a labored reading style with much lip movement.

Teachers do not have to follow the program rigidly, but they may use it in an ongoing program. Some experts comment that this approach has been found to be successful when it is used with modifications.

Mathematics Disorders

Bellugi (1988) tells us that the brain's mathematic-arithmetic system is located in the same hemisphere as spoken, gestural, and other language symbols.

Reading and arithmetic are similar in many ways; numbers and words stand for concepts, rule systems govern the correct use of the numbers and words, etc. (Kirk, Gallagher & Anastasiow, 1993). A child with a language problem is very likely to have difficulty in calculating.

The author has used the following math program effectively in remediating problems with learning disabled children.

Keymath (Connelly, 1988) is a diagnostic math test. It is an individually administered, norm-referenced device. This test is appropriate for a wide range of grade levels (K–9). The most important thing about Keymath is that Connolly (1992) published a remedial math kit to remediate math problems after the test has been administered. *Keymath Teach and Practice for Operations* (TAP–OP) is an update of *Keymath Teach and Practice: Activities for the Diagnosis and Remediation of Computational Difficulties* (1985). TAP–OP provides prescriptive skills in four areas of math.

Writing Disorders

The child who has reading problems will often have writing and spelling problems. A child with motor problems may need the help of an occupational therapist to help with the writing problems. Most children have problems with the mechanics of grammar and not the physical properties of writing.

Underlying language problems are often expressed in writing and spelling problems as well as reading difficulties.

Is There a Single Cause?

No one, to date, has discovered a single cause for learning disabilities. Satz, Morrison & Fletcher (1985) identified the following sub-groups that are trouble areas and possible causes of learning disabilities:

Nonverbal communication
Learning strategies
Short-term memory
Maturational pace (hence a lag in development)
Processing verbal information
Perceptual process—auditory or visual
Motor control; impulsivity
Neurological structures
Motivation
Genes or generic disorders

REFERENCES

American Psychiatric Association. (1987). *Diagnostic and statistical manual of mental disorders* (3rd ed.). Washington, DC.

Badian, N. (1982). The prediction of good and poor reading before kindergarten entry: A four-year follow-up. *Journal of Special Education, 16,* 309–318.

Badian, N. (1988). The prediction of good and poor reading before kindergarten entry: A nine-year follow-up. *Journal of Learning Disabilities, 21,* 98–103, 123.

Bannatyne, A. (1974). Diagnosis: A note on recategorization on the WISC scaled scores. *Journal of Learning Disabilities, 7,* 272–273.

Barkley, R. A. (1981a). *Hyperactive children: A handbook for diagnosis and treatment.* New York: Guilford Press.

Barkley, R. A. (1981c). Learning disabilities. In E. Mash & L. Terdal (Eds.), *Behavioral assessment of childhood disorders* (pp. 441–482). New York: Guilford Press.

Bellugi, U. (1988). *Language development. The mind* (Vol. 7). New York: WNET, Educational Broadcasting.

Bond, G., & Tinker, M. (1967). *Reading difficulties: Their diagnosis and correction.* New York: Appleton-Century-Crofts.

Chalfant, J. (1985). Identifying learning disabled students: A summary of the national task force report. *Learning Disabilities Focus, 1,* 9–20.

Clark, D. B. (1988). *Dyslexia: Theory and practice of remedial instruction.* Parkton, MD: York Press.

Clements, S. D., & Peters, J. (1962). Specific Learning Disabilities: An Attentional Deficit Syndrome. In H. Myklebust (Ed.), *Progress in learning disabilities (Vol. II)*, pp. 56–93. New York: Grune and Straton.

Connolly, A. (1988). *Keymath Revised: A Diagnostic Inventory of Essential Mathematics.* Circle Pines, MN: American Guidance Service.

Curtis, S., & Tallal, P. (1991). On the nature of impairment in language in children. In J. Miller (Ed.), *New directions in research on child language disorders*, pp. 189–210. Boston: College Hill Press.

Deshler, D., & Schumaker, J. (1983). Social skills of learning disabled adolescents: A review of characteristics and interventions. *Topics in Learning and Learning Disabilities, 3,* 15–32.

Ekwall, E., & Shanker, J. (1988). *Diagnosis and remediation of the disabled reader* (3rd ed.). Boston: Allyn & Bacon.

Federal Register. (1977). Nondiscriminatory on Basis of Handicap, May 4, pp. 22, 676-22, 702. Washington, DC: Author.

Fisher, J. A. (1910). Congenital word blindness, trans. *Ophthalmological Society United Kingdom, 30,* 216.

Goodman, K. (1976). Reading: A psycholinguistic guessing game. In H. Singer & R. Rudel (Eds.), *Theoretical models of processing of reading*, pp. 497–505. Newark, NJ: International Reading Association.

Hallahan, D., & Kauffman, J. (1991). *Exceptional children.* Englewood Cliffs, NJ: Prentice Hall.

Hardman, M., Drew, C., Egan, W., & Wolf, B. (1993). *Human exceptionality* (4th ed.). Boston: Allyn & Bacon.

Harris, A. (1961). *How to increase reading ability* (4th ed.). New York: David McKay.

Individuals with Disabilities Education Act of 1990. (1990). USC, Chapter 3, p. 20.

Interagency Committee. (1990). *Learning disabilities: A report to Congress.* Washington, D.C.: U.S. Government Printing Office.

Kavale, K., Forness, S., & Bender, M. (Eds.). (1987). *Handbook of learning disabilities: Vol. 1, Dimensions and diagnoses; Vol. 2, Methods and intervention; Vol. 3, Programs and practices.* Boston: College-Hill/Little, Brown.

Kirk, S. (1966). *Personal communication.*

Kirk, S., Gallagher, J., & Anastasiow, N. (1993). *Educating exceptional children.* Boston: Houghton Mifflin.

Levine, M. (1980). *A pediatric approach to learning disorders.* New York: Wiley.

Liberman, I. Y., & Liverman, A. M. (1990). Whole language versus code emphasis. *Annals of Dyslexia, 40,* 51–75.

Love, H. D., & Litton, F. W. (1994). *Teaching reading to disabled and handicapped learners.* Springfield, IL: Charles C Thomas.

McGee, R., Williams, S., & Silva, P. A. (1987). A comparison of girls and boys with teacher-identified problems of attention. *Journal of Childhood and Adolescent Psychiatry, 26,* 711–717.

Miller, M., Stoneburger, R. L., & Brecht, R. D. (1978). WISC subtest patterns as discriminators of perceptual disability. *Journal of Learning Disabilities, 11,* 449–452.

Myklebust, H. (1968). Learning Disabilities: Definition and Overview. In *Progress in learning disabilities*, Vol. 1, pp. 1–15. New York: Grune & Stratton.

National Joint Committee for Learning Disabilities. (1991). *A statement of the National Joint Committee for Learning Disabilities*, pp. 15–16.

Orton, S. (1937). *Reading, writing and speech problems of children.* New York: Norton.

Rourke, B. (Ed.). (1991). *Neurological validation of learning disability subtypes.* New York: Guilford Press.

Sattler, J. (1988). *Assessment of children* (3rd ed.). San Diego: J.M. Sattler.

Satz, M., Morrison, H., & Fletcher, L. (1985). Learning disability subtypes: A review. In F. J. Pirozzolo & M. C. Wittock (Eds.), *Neuropsychological and cognitive processes in reading*, pp. 109–144. New York: Academic Press.

Schumaker, J. B., Deshler, D. D., & McKnight, R. C. (1991). Teaching routines for content areas at the secondary level. In G. Stover, M. R. Shinn, & H. M. Walker (Eds.), *Intervention for achievement and behavior problems*, pp. 473–494. Washington, D.C.: National Association of School Psychologists.

Torgesen, J. K., & Kail, R. V. (1980). Memory processes in exceptional children. In B. K. Keogh (Ed.), *Advances in special education, Vol. 1: Basic constructs and theoretical orientations.* Greenwich, CT: J.A.I. Press.

U.S. Department of Education. (1977). *Sixth annual report to Congress on the implementation of PL 94-142: The Education of All Handicapped Children Act.* Washington, D.C.: U.S. Government Printing Office.

U.S. Department of Education. (1991). *Thirteenth annual report to Congress on the implementation of Education of the Handicapped Act.* Washington, D.C.: Division of Educational Services, Special Education Programs.

Wechsler, David. (1991). *Wechsler intelligence scale for children manual* (3rd ed.). San Antonio: Psychological Corp., Harcourt Brace Jovanovich.

Chapter 5

EMOTIONAL AND BEHAVIORAL DISORDERS

In America, every day, 1,293 teenagers will give birth; 6 teens will commit suicide; 1,849 children will be abused; 3,288 children will run away from home; 1,629 children will be incarcerated in adult jails; and 2,989 children will see their parents divorce (Children's Defense Fund, 1989).

The school dropout rate for students with behavior disorders is over 40 percent. Fewer than half are placed in integrated settings. When these students exit secondary schools, about one-third are neither working nor engaged in any employment-related training (Peacock Hill Working Group, 1990).

Too many children are not growing up healthy, resilient, and skilled. Violence, poverty, poor health, teen parenthood, and school failure dim the future of children. When the future of our children is dimmed, the lives of all Americans are diminished (Center for the Study of Social Policy, 1990).

There is a very large group of children having school problems who are screaming at educators with their behaviors. They are saying that school is not relevant, is boring and dull, and not meeting their needs and literally driving them crazy. These students drop out, form gangs, get in trouble, and yet society will not look at itself and the school system for creative answers and alternatives (Forest and Pearpoint, 1990, p. 188).

Referring to a 1989 report released by the Institute of Medicine, Yale University, Dr. Frederick Solomon, Director of the Mental Health Division, noted that for emotionally disturbed children, "the evidence is that less than 30 and maybe less than 20 percent are served."

DEFINITIONS

It is not an easy task to define behavior and emotional problems in children. Kirk, Gallagher, and Anastasiow (1993) tell us that:

most definitions assume that a child with a behavior disorder, or serious emotional disturbance, reveals consistent age-inappropriate behavior leading to social conflict, personal unhappiness, and school failure. But almost all children reveal age-inappropriate behavior at one time or another. Moreover, a child's behavior is not the only variable that determines classification in this category. The person who perceives the child's behavior as "inappropriate" plays a key role in the decision. Clearly, some kinds of behavior such as physical attacks, constant weeping or unhappiness, and extreme hyperactivity are unacceptable in any setting. But the acceptability of a wide range of other behaviors depends on the attitude of the perceiver.

In the pluralistic society in which we live, behavior that is acceptable in some groups or subcultures is unacceptable in others. Our definition, therefore, must allow for cultural differences. We cannot define a child as deviant if the child's behavior is the norm in the child's cultural group, even though we find the particular behavior as socially unacceptable (p. 410).

Wood (1982) suggested that a definition should include four elements:

1. *The disturber element.* What or who is perceived to be the focus of the problem?
2. *The problem behavior element.* How is the problem behavior described?
3. *The setting element.* In what setting does the problem occur?
4. *The disturbed element.* Who regards the behavior as a problem? (pp. 7–8)

These elements suggest an environmental basis for the definition of problem behavior. It is not just the behavior but the context in which the behavior is observed.

VARIABLES IN BEHAVIOR DISORDERS

Hardman, Drew, Egan & Wolf (1993) suggest that:

Many variables influence the types of behaviors that are exhibited or suppressed by individuals with behavior disorders. These include the parents' and teachers' management styles; the school or home environment; the social and cultural values of the family; the social and economic climate of the community; the responses of peers and siblings; and the academic, intellectual, and social-emotional characteristics of the individuals with the disorders.

A number of terms have been used to describe individuals with emotional, social, and behavior problems. These terms include behavior disorders, social maladjustment, emotional disturbance, seriously emotionally disturbed, and others.

Forness (1992) summarized the key elements in the federal law (PL 94–142):

1. An inability to learn that cannot be explained by intellectual, sensory, or health factors

2. An inability to build or maintain satisfactory relationships with peers and teachers
3. Inappropriate types of behaviors or feelings under normal circumstances
4. A general pervasive mood of unhappiness or depression
5. A tendency to develop physical symptoms or fears associated with personal or school problems. (p. 55)

In addition to these five individual characteristics, the definition of SED also includes the criteria of extensive duration of the problem, severity of the problem, and demonstrated adverse effect on school performance. Excluded from this group are children and youths who are socially maladjusted but not emotionally maladjusted. The socially maladjusted child is excluded from special education services.

Kirk, Gallagher & Anastasiow (1993) give an example of Pete, a twelve year old doing quite poorly in school (third or fourth grade proficiency).

> He is a constant trial to his teachers in the middle school. He physically attacks other students when frustrated (which seems to be quite often), is suspected of being a part of a group of older boys stealing from local stores, and is openly defiant to the teacher in the classroom.
>
> The teachers don't have any trouble reaching the conclusion that Pete needs some special attention, with social skills training perhaps leading the list. But the school psychologist has trouble fitting him under the general category of seriously emotionally disturbed as just defined because Pete doesn't reveal a pervasive mood of unhappiness or depression. His role in life appears to be to upset other people. He can, without a doubt, be called socially maladjusted; but is he "socially maladjusted without emotional disturbance" and, hence, excluded from special education services? (p. 412)

This type of bureaucracy or getting around the problem infuriates teachers but is the result of the eligibility requirements in the Education for All Handicapped Children Act (PL 94–142).

The above described definition of severe emotional disturbance or behavior disorders was derived from an earlier definition by Bower (1959). Hardman, Drew, Egan, and Wolf (1993) tell us that Bower's definition has been severely criticized because of its lack of clarity, incompleteness, and exclusion of individuals described as socially maladjusted. Additionally, in order for students to be served under this definition, assessment personnel must demonstrate that the disorder is adversely affecting students' school performance. In many cases, students with serious behavior disorders—such as eating disorders, depression, suicidal tendencies, and social withdrawal—do not receive appropriate care and treatment merely because their academic achievement in school appears to be normal or above average. In some cases, the students are gifted (p. 136).

Recently, committees and coalitions from a variety of professional health and educational organizations have proposed a new definition and terminology for *serious emotional disturbance* for federal legislation in the United States (Council for Exceptional Children, 1991; Forness & Knitzer, 1990):

> Emotional or Behavior Disorders (EBD) refers to a condition in which behavioral or emotional responses of an individual in school are so different from his/her generally accepted, age-appropriate, ethnic, or cultural norms that they adversely affect educational performance in such areas as self-care, social relationships, personal adjustment, academic progress, classroom behavior, or work adjustment.
>
> EBD is more than a transient expected response to stressors in the child's or youth's environment and would persist even with individualized interventions, such as feedback to the individual, consultation with parents or families, and/or modification of the educational environment.
>
> The eligibility decision must be based on multiple sources of data about the individual's behavioral or emotional functioning. EBD must be exhibited in at least two different settings, at least one of which must be school related.
>
> EBD can co-exist with other handicapping conditions as defined elsewhere in this law [IDEA].
>
> This category may include children or youth with schizophrenia, affective disorders, or with other sustained disturbances of conduct, attention or adjustment (Council for Exceptional Children, 1991, p. 10).

We are told by Hardman, Drew, Egan, and Wolf (1993) that:

> Features of this newly proposed definition represent significant advantages over the present federal definition, including (1) the inclusion of impairments of adaptive behavior as evidenced in emotional, social, or behavioral differences; (2) the use of normative standards of assessment from multiple sources, including consideration of cultural and/or ethnic factors; (3) the examination of prereferral interventions and other efforts to assist children prior to formally classifying them as disabled; and (4) the potential inclusion of individuals previously labeled socially maladjusted (p. 136).

PREVALENCE

Knitzer (1982) estimated the prevalence of serious emotional disturbances at 5 percent, or about three million children. On the other hand, Stroul and Friedman (1986) estimated that 11.8 percent of children had emotional disturbance. Actually, the range of estimates can extend from 1 percent to more than 20 percent of the school-age population (Paul &

Epanchin, 1986). Perhaps the most serious figure, though, is the one that indicates that less than 1 percent of children with this description are receiving special services (Twelfth Annual Report to Congress, Office of Special Education Programs, U.S. Department of Education, 1990).

Rather consistently credible studies in the United States and many other countries of the world have indicated that at least 6 to 10 percent of children and youth of school age exhibit serious and persistent emotional/behavioral problems (Institute of Medicine, 1989; Kazdin, 1989).

Kirk, Gallagher, and Anastasiow (1993) have this to say about the discrepancy:

> When estimates of prevalence differ by millions of children, a problem with operationalizing the concept is indicated. The federal definition says the presence of an inability to build or maintain satisfactory interpersonal relationships with peers and teachers, or a general pervasive mood of unhappiness or depression — that is present to a marked degree, marks the seriously emotionally disturbed child; but who decided what "a marked degree" is or what "pervasive" means? (p. 413).

CLASSIFICATIONS

Forness and Kavale (1988), Swartz, Mosley, and Koenig-Jerz (1987) tell us there is no consistent use of a standard set of criteria for determining the nature and severity of behavior disorders. If we did have eligibility and classification systems, they would provide educational, psychological, and psychiatric clinicians with extremely valuable information about the nature of conditions, effective treatment, and other important information.

A classification system would serve many purposes for human services workers. It would provide, for example, a common set of terms for communicating with others. An example would be Down syndrome children, who share some rather distinct characteristics. Physicians and other health workers use these characteristics and other information for diagnosing and treating these children.

STATISTICALLY DERIVED CLASSIFICATION SYSTEM

While we do not have a classification system, some researchers (Quay, 1975, 1979; Von Isser, Quay & Love, 1980) have identified four distinct categories of behavior disorders in children:

1. Conduct disorders involve such characteristics as overt aggression, both verbal and physical; disruptiveness, negativism, irresponsibility; and defiance of authority— all of which are at variance with the behavioral expectations of the school and other social institutions.
2. Anxiety-withdrawal stands in considerable contrast to conduct disorders, involving, as it does, overanxiety, social withdrawal, seclusiveness, shyness, sensitivity, and other behaviors implying a retreat from the environment rather than a hostile response to it.
3. Immaturity characteristically involves preoccupation, short attention span, passivity, daydreaming, sluggishness, and other behavior not in accord with developmental expectations.
4. Socialized aggression typically involves gang activities, cooperative stealing, truancy, and other manifestations of participation in a delinquent subculture. (Von Isser et al., 1980, pp. 272–273)

CLINICALLY DERIVED CLASSIFICATION SYSTEMS

The system most used by psychological and medical professionals is the American Psychiatric Associations (1987) Diagnostic and Statistical Manual of Mental Disorders (3rd ed. rev.) (DSM–III–R).

The DSM–III–R identifies nine major groups of disorders which may be exhibited by infants, children or adolescents. They are (1) developmental disorders, (2) disruptive behavior disorders, (3) anxiety disorders of childhood or adolescence, (4) eating disorders, (5) gender identity disorders, (6) tic disorders, (7) elimination disorders, (8) speech disorders, and (9) other disorders of infancy, childhood, or adolescence.

Table 5.1 lists the diagnostic criteria for conduct disorder and the criteria for severity of the conduct disorder.

CLASSIFICATION ACCORDING TO SEVERITY

Children may exhibit characteristic types of behavior with varying degrees of intensity or severity. The classification of the severe disorders are typically called childhood psychoses or pervasive developmental disorders. We used to call these people crazy or insane.

TYPES OF CHILDHOOD PSYCHOSIS

Two types of childhood psychoses are distinguished by most researchers: **autism** and **childhood schizophrenia.** Children with autism are characterized by a lack of responsiveness to other people, major problems in communication (many do not have any useful language), peculiar speech patterns (such as parroting what they hear), and bizarre responses (e.g., peculiar interests in or attachment to objects). They often engage in

Table 5.1
Diagnostic Criteria for Conduct Disorder

```
A.  A disturbance of conduct lasting at least six
    months, during which at least three of the following
    have been present:
    ( 1) Has stolen without confrontation of a
         victim on more than one occasion
         (including forgery)
    ( 2) Has run away from home overnight at least
         twice while living in parental or
         parental-surrogate home (or once without
         returning)
    ( 3) Often lies (other than to avoid physical
         or sexual abuse)
    ( 4) Has deliberately engaged in fire-setting
    ( 5) Is often truant from school (for older
         person, absent from work)
    ( 6) Has broken into someone else's home,
         building, or car
    ( 7) Has deliberately destroyed other's
         property (other than by fire-setting)
    ( 8) Has been physically cruel to animals
    ( 9) Has forced someone into sexual activity
         with him or her
    (10) Has used a weapon in more than one fight
    (11) Often initiates physical fights
    (12) Has stolen with confrontation of a victim
         (e.g., mugging, purse-snatching,
         extortion, armed robbery)
    (13) Has been physically cruel to people

B.  If 18 or older, does not meet criteria for
    Antisocial Disorder.

Criteria for Severity of Conduct Disorder:
    Mild:  Few if any problems in excess of those
    required to make the diagnosis, and conduct problems
    cause only minor harm to others.
    Moderate:  Number of conduct problems and effect on
    others intermediate between "mild" and "severe."
    Severe:  Many conduct problems in excess of those
    required to make the diagnosis, or conduct problems
    cause considerable harm to others, e.g., serious
    physical injury to victims, extensive vandalism or
    theft, prolonged absence from home.
```

repetitive, stereotyped behavior. Children with schizophrenia have a severe disorder of thinking. They may believe that they are controlled by alien forces or have other delusions or hallucinations. Typically, their emotions are inappropriate for the actual circumstances, and they tend to withdraw into a private world.

One major difference between autism and schizophrenia is that a child with autism is typically recognized as having a disorder before the age of thirty months. Childhood schizophrenia is a disorder that generally begins after a normal period of development, usually longer than thirty months. Autism and schizophrenia in children, then, are differentiated partly on the basis of the child's age at the first appearance of symptoms. There are other differences between the two conditions: (1) Children with schizophrenia usually have delusions (bizarre ideas) and hallucinations (seeing or hearing imaginary things), whereas children with autism usually do not; (2) children with schizophrenia tend to have psychotic episodes interspersed with periods of near normal behavior, whereas children with autism tend to have persistent symptoms; (3) about 25 percent of children with autism have epileptic seizures, whereas children with schizophrenia seldom have seizures.

CAUSES

What do we mean by causes? Very often the cause of behavior disorders can never be adequately determined. In many cases, there is a multitude of causes for the behavior disorder of a specific child.

It is fortunate for us that effective intervention is possible even when the initial causes of behavior disorders are not known. As a matter of fact, even when the causes may have little relevance for effective intervention, it is good for the practitioner to know them. For instance, many contributory conditions such as brain damage or severe child abuse involve historical events that cannot be undone, yet effective intervention can reduce or eliminate the impairments.

It would take several pages of this book to list every condition that has been suggested at one time or another by psychologists, physicians, teachers, etc. as a cause of behavior disorders. However, it is fortunate for us that these factors fall into just a few categories. Research points to a number of biological and psychological conditions that are important determinants of a child's development, both normal and in many cases abnormal. Second, there are several models of behavior disorders. For example, the psychoeducational, behavioral, and ecological models are of particular relevance. Each of these models involves certain ideas about how behavior disorders are produced and each provides intervention principles that we have been using in special education. Table 5.2 is a summary of the various causes of behavior disorders in children and adolescents.

Table 5.2
Summary of Causes of Behavior Disorders

(1) **Biological**
A *biogenic mental disorder* is a severe behavior disorder that results solely from the effects of biological factors, including both gene action and the effects of the physical-chemical environment. (Rimland, 1969, p. 706)

(2) **Psychodynamic**
A child suffers *emotional conflict* whenever anything interferes with the satisfaction of his instinctual drives and his frustration produces a state of tension. (Lippman, 1962, p. 3)

(3) **Behavioral**
Psychological disorder is said to be present when a child emits behavior that deviates from an arbitrary and relative social norm in that it occurs with a frequency or intensity that authoritative adults in the child's environment judge, under the circumstances, to be either too high or too low. (Ross, 1980, p. 9)

(4) **Ecological**
Emotional disturbance [is] a reciprocal condition which exists when intense coping responses are released within a human community by a community member's atypical behavior and responses. The triggering stimulus, the rejoinder of the microcommunity, and the ensuing transaction are all involved in emotional disturbance. (Rhodes, 1970, p. 311)

(5) **Educational**
Behavioral disorders of a student are behavior characteristics that (a) deviate from educators' standards of normality and (b) impair the functioning of that student and/or others. These behavior characteristics are manifested as environmental conflicts and/or personal disturbances and are typically accompanied by learning disorders. (Cullinan, Epstein, & Lloyd, 1983)

BIOLOGICAL FACTORS

Behavior may be influenced by genetic, neurological, or biochemical factors or, in many cases, a combination of these. There is certainly a relationship between body and behavior and it seems reasonable that we should look for a biological causal factor of some kind for certain emotional and behavior disorders. Only rarely, though, is it possible to demonstrate a relationship between a specific biological factor and E/BD.

Many children with E/BD do not have detectable biological flaws that would account for their inappropriate actions, and many children with normal behavior have serious biological defects. For most children, though, particularly the ones with E/BD, there simply is no concrete evidence that biological factors are alone at the root of the problem. For children with severe and profound disorders, however, there is some evidence to suggest that biological factors do play a part in the condition.

Children are born with a biologically determined behavioral style and we call it temperament. Although a child's inborn temperament can be changed by the way he/she is reared, some believe that children have problems with temperaments that are predisposed to develop E/BD. However, there is no relationship between temperament and E/BD that can be proven statistically. A child who is difficult may be handled as well as a child with easy temperament. There are other biological factors besides temperament and some of these are disease, brain trauma, malnutrition, and drug abuse that may cause a child to develop emotional problems. Substance abuse, it has been found, can contribute to serious emotional and behavioral problems.

We know, in the case of mental retardation, that there is a great deal of evidence of a biological cause that is the reason for severe and profoundly disabled children. Psychotic children, the ones who are autistic or schizophrenic, don't always show signs of inborn neurological defects. There is convincing evidence that genetic factors do play a large role in schizophrenia. It is now generally accepted by people in the mental health field that autism is a neurological disorder, but that the nature and causes of the neurological defect are unknown.

FAMILY FACTORS

The people who work in the mental health units sometimes attempt to blame behavioral problems primarily on the parents' relationship with the child. We say that the father and mother have a profound influence on early development, and that is true. In fact, some advocates of psychoanalysis believe that all severe problems of children come about because of the interaction between the mother and the child. Evidence, though, indicates that the family does influence the child a great deal, but that deviant children may influence their parents as much as the parents influence them. We have children from religious homes who become emotionally disturbed. We have children from extremely dysfunctional homes, from low socioeconomic levels, who appear to be fairly well adjusted and go on to be hugely successful in life. Even in cases of severe and profound E/BD, it is not possible to find a consistent and valid cause for the child's problem as far as it being placed primarily on the parents. Family discipline plays a part in the outcome of the child, but once again, we can find nothing consistent about family discipline that causes behavioral problems in children. There are probably as many routes to becoming a good parent when it comes to discipline as there are routes of becoming a poor parent. In other words, some parents employ very strict and harsh discipline and it does not seem to harm the children. Other parents who employ the same type discipline have children who grow up to have a behavior disorder. The same can be said of parents who have very lax discipline. Some children from such homes grow up to be emotionally disturbed and some children from such homes grow up to be well adjusted, producing citizens. We know one thing for sure, environmental influences do not operate on a family by family basis, but on an individual by individual basis.

CULTURAL FACTORS

Other than family and school, many environmental conditions affect the parents' expectations of their children and their children's expectations for themselves, their siblings, and their peers. Values and behavioral standards are communicated to children through a variety of cultural ways. Several cultural influences come to mind, and the author is thinking of children who grow up in an area where there is war. These children seem to be anxious and scared much of the time, but when the war is over, they tend to forget about it. We also know that children who grow up in strictly religious societies are affected by the way that people react to their religions and are affected by the way they react to their religions. Children who grow up in violent areas such as inner-cities, where there is much gang life, tend to believe that the things they do are okay because members of their inner society accept the things they do as being okay. Some of these children are surprised to learn people outside their culture find the things they do horribly wrong. We also know that in America, culture is affecting some children adversely. There is a dramatic increase in the number of children living in poverty. There have also been substantial increases in the number of children born of teenage mothers and to mothers who are drug addicts. At the same time, we are cutting medical and social services available to poor children in

America and this seems to have an important impact on the mental health, not only of the children, but of their parents.

SCHOOL FACTORS

Some children have already become emotionally disturbed by the time they begin school. Others develop behavioral disorders during their school years. The ones who develop the disorders during their school years could have the disorder because of damaging experiences in the classroom itself. Some children will become emotionally disturbed because of a combination of the experiences in the classroom and the experiences at home. It is a fact, though, that very few first graders are emotionally disturbed. As children go through school, behavior problems and emotional maladjustment increase significantly. By the time the children get to the junior high school level, there are significant numbers of them with behavioral and emotional problems. This would leave the author to believe that there are experiences within the school, but most probably in the home environment and among the peers of the children that cause the behavioral disorders to increase with time.

STATISTICAL TECHNIQUES

When we use checklists, rating scales, and other measuring devices to evaluate large numbers of children, we can often pinpoint and sort-out clusters of responses that separate one group of symptoms from another. Quay & Werry (1986) state that this approach has yielded four patterns of deviant behavior in children: conduct disorders, anxiety-withdrawal, immaturity, and socialized aggression. The following was presented in a book by Kirk, Gallagher, & Anastasiow (1993):

1. Children who have a conduct disorder defy authority, are hostile toward authoritative figures (police officers, teachers); are cruel, malicious, and assaultive; and have few guilt feelings. This group includes children who are hyperactive, restless, and hyperkinetic.
2. The **anxiety-withdrawal** classification includes children who are shy, timid, seclusive, sensitive, and submissive. They are overdependent and easily depressed. According to Quay and Werry's study, these children come mostly from overprotective families in the higher socioeconomic levels.
3. The **immaturity** dimension refers to children who are inattentive, sluggish, uninterested in school, lazy, preoccupied, and reticent. They appear to be less able to function in the regular classroom than are children who are anxious or who have conduct disorders.
4. Children in the **socialized-aggression** classification share certain charac-

teristics with those with conduct disorders (such as hostility, aggression, few guilt feelings), but are socialized within their peer group, usually a gang. Common behaviors for these youngsters include stealing and truancy. Although these behaviors may not be considered maladaptive within the specific environment in which these children exist, they do present a clear danger to the larger society.

The term *social maladjustment* would seem to cover both conduct disorders and socialized-aggressive behavior in this categorization, but these problems emerge from different sources and this may even separate them in terms of eligibility for services.

CONDUCT DISORDERS

There is a common pattern in the families of children with conduct disorders. We find, very often, that the father is aggressive and hostile and uses physical force when he disciplines the children. In the case of Johnny, a young child who was in the sixth grade, his father treated what he thought was Johnny's misbehavior by spanking him, almost like beatings. This indicates that Johnny's father had a lot of hostility. It is often said by authorities that hostility breeds hostility and, therefore, Johnny became even more of a problem when later his mother and father divorced. We find that the mothers in these families tend to try to get along because of financial survival. Also, they will discipline the children one day, and the next day will not discipline them for exactly the same offense. We know that the entire family could benefit from treatment and some attempts have been made to involve all members of the family in treatment.

There are many different theories concerning the causes of aggressive behavior typical of the conduct disorders we find. One theory is based on social learning theory and has gained wide acceptance. It has been argued over and over again that children with conduct disorders, especially boys, learn that aggressive behavior is a way of getting what they want. If they see this aggressive behavior in their parents, then they become aggressive when they need to get something they want. They use this response over and over again in different situations, usually getting their way. Parental punishment is often ineffective and sporadic and only provides another model of aggressiveness. These children often are rewarded for their aggressive behavior and, therefore, they continue this type of behavior. There is a small group of children who have a neurological disorder that is at the root of this aggressive behavior, but several authorities say this group makes up only about 5 percent of children with conduct disorders with neurological disorders as the cause. This condition tends to run in families because the children who learn to be aggressive also teach their own children to be aggressive. Educators have become more directly involved with these children lately because they generally score lower in academics than other children.

There are many problems associated with asocial and antisocial behavior, and unless these problems are dealt with vigorously in childhood, they will lead to antisocial behavior in adulthood. This could potentially create a generation of antisocial children who become antisocial adults and the cycle continues.

ANXIETY, WITHDRAWAL, AND IMMATURITY

There are many children who are anxious or withdrawn and they are a bigger threat to themselves than to others around them. These children are usually not disruptive and they generally do not cause classroom management problems. However, they should be a source of worry for teachers. We can contrast these children with those having conduct disorders because these children show too little and the ones with conduct disorders show too much. Their problems are with excessive internal control; they maintain firm control over their impulses by being anxious and withdrawn. These children are rigid and unable to be spontaneous.

Let's take the case of a little girl named Jane. She has learned helplessness and is a failure time after time because she keeps saying to herself, "I cannot do this." The children around her often try to get her to do things, but she feels worthless and helpless, and in the face of other children and an unfriendly environment, she withdraws into herself. Jane's poor performance in the classroom may be much worse than she is capable of doing, primarily because she is so pessimistic about her ability. This little girl has very low self-esteem, and the underachievement of children like her is because other people have not helped them gain self-esteem. Therefore, they become anxious, and as they get more anxious, they withdraw.

We can ask ourselves about where fearful children come from? Well, we know that many of these children have parents with similar problems. Also, we know that children with chronic anxiety don't know how to get out of stressful situations and they don't know how to go about improving their lives. The inability of these children to change tends to add to their feelings of helplessness. This reinforces low self-esteem.

A serious outcome of intense periods of anxiety, withdrawal, and depression is suicide. Suicide is a very big problem among college students and teenagers between the ages of 16 and 18. What do we look for? How can we tell if a child is suicidal? Kirk, Gallagher, and Anastasiow cite Paul and Epanchin (1986) who described five danger signs:

1. A suicide threat or statement or behavior indicating a wish or intention to die
2. A previous suicide attempt
3. Mental depression
4. Marked changes in behavior, personality, or both
5. Making final arrangements (for example, giving away prized possessions; p. 308)

Guetzloe (1988) states that a teacher who sees these signs in children has the immediate task of providing the student's relief from the feelings of helplessness and hopelessness. Some positive change, however small, must be made to prove to the student that the situation is not hopeless. This often makes a noticeable difference. Long-range treatment for a student may demand a variety of services from community and mental health agencies, and teachers should be aware that there are generally good referral sources in the community. For schools, the best method of prevention is an educational program. This program must enhance the feelings of self-worth and self-control in children.

INTERVENTIONS—APPROACHES TO TREATMENT

Interventions for children and adolescents who have behavior disorders include a variety of approaches. The major approaches to treatment include insight-oriented therapy, play therapy, group psychotherapy, behavior therapy, marital and family therapy, and drug therapy. Unfortunately, many of these therapies are not available to students who live in small to moderate size cities. As a rule, school systems do not have therapists who can work with these children. Many of the therapists are found in the community working for mental health agencies and will work with students after school and on the weekends.

INSIGHT-ORIENTED THERAPY

Insight-oriented therapy includes psychoanalytic, nondirective, and client-centered therapy. These approaches assume that the child who feels rejection, guilt, and even rage can be helped by an understanding and caring therapist. The therapist tries to establish a relationship with the child by creating an atmosphere that is conducive to expressing feelings. The goal of therapy is to help the child develop better mechanisms to deal with his problems. These mechanisms will provide relief of symptoms and he can then develop more adaptive behaviors.

PLAY THERAPY

Play therapy is for young children and serves several purposes. It is to help the child become aware of his own unconscious feelings that are tearing him apart. The therapist will give the child a situation and let the child engage in play fantasizing. It is believed that the child will tell his problem when he engages in the play. Through play therapy, children reveal information that the therapist can then use as valuable information to help alleviate the child's problems.

GROUP PSYCHOTHERAPY

Group psychotherapy and other group-oriented treatments are used only occasionally with children and then with older children. A group of children or adolescents meets with a therapist and they begin talking out their problems. It is believed that all the children can help each other solve the problems of individuals in the group. The therapist is there to guide them in the discussions.

BEHAVIOR THERAPY

Behavioral interventions for children focus on developing various self-help, social, language, and academic behaviors. This is called principles of behavior modification in many settings. Rewards or token reinforcement systems are some of the things that are used in behavior therapy. The idea is to get the child to change his behavior and then he is rewarded for doing so.

Another focus of behavioral intervention is the reduction or elimination of maladaptive behavior. The idea is for a therapist to talk to boys, for example, who have been fighting constantly and reward them if they stop fighting. Every time a boy gets into a fight, the therapist talks to him and tries to reinforce the idea that this is the wrong type of behavior. Tokens may be given in this type of reinforcement also.

MARITAL AND FAMILY THERAPY

If parents are having marital problems, then often their children have problems. The parents must seek marital therapy on their own, but they can be told by the school system that their problems are hurting their child. If the parents do not choose to seek marital therapy, there is nothing the school can do to make them. However, when parents do seek therapy, very often the child is helped because he feels a part of solving the total problem.

DRUG THERAPY

Physicians often prescribe various drugs to help children for a variety of conditions and related behaviors. Children who are hyperactive, inattentive, and impulsive sometimes are treated with stimulant drugs. Children and youth with severe behavior problems are often treated with medications to control disorganized or highly erratic behavior. In some cases, medications are prescribed for children who have chronic problems with bedwetting or involuntary urination. Older teenagers or young adults may be prescribed drugs that are ordinarily taken by adults to alleviate depression or other psychiatric conditions.

EARLY CHILDHOOD INTERVENTIONS

There are several service delivery systems that we use to help disturbed young children. However, four systems are generally used to provide children who are disturbed with necessary services used: (1) home-based program, (2) home-based program followed by a specialized center, (3) home- and center-based system, and (4) center-based program.

The home-based program approach provides disturbed children with specialized services through a home teacher. The teacher will train the parent to use behavior modification and other therapeutic procedures. The parents then employ these techniques to help their children in learning and mastering new and appropriate behavior skills. Home-based behavioral interventions seem to produce good results in young children who have conduct disorders.

The referrals for home-based service programs generally come from physicians, school guidance personnel, public school personnel, and county health nurses. Home teachers assist parents in selecting the appropriate goals for their children which are based on actual performance data that someone has observed in the child firsthand. The person who has observed these things in the child firsthand is often the parent or the home teacher. The home-based program consists of helping the child in the areas of self-help, language, socialization, and motor skills.

The home-based program is often followed by a specialized center program. The intent of these programs is to provide a carefully conceived,

sequential program in which objectives for the home and center programs are interrelated. In general, children who are served at home from
birth to approximately three years by a home teacher will then start
going to a program away from home. The home-teacher continues to
serve the child, but the child is also sent to a center where trained
personnel help the child to overcome his problems. We go then from a
home-based program to a combination home-base/special facility program.
Teachers and therapists alike work with the child to try to change his
bad behavior patterns.

Finally, we have the center-based program which is exclusively used.
The parents send the child to a special center each day for services by
trained personnel in helping the child to overcome his bad behavior
patterns. This is sometimes an expensive program and the cost is shared
by parents and the public school system. There are therapists available
to help the child in the center along with teachers and other school
personnel.

INTERVENTIONS FOR ELEMENTARY-AGED CHILDREN

The elementary school children with behavior disorders are likely to
exhibit below average performance in reading and math as well as other
typical school curriculum. In addition to their academic problems, they
often have trouble getting along with peers and teachers.

The academic problems are often addressed in remedial programs.
The behavior problems are sometimes addressed in the classroom through
behavior modification, but also the teacher has personnel such as guidance counselors, school psychologists, school nurses, and even physicians
to help at various times. The largest school systems will have many more
personnel available for help than the moderate and small town schools.

Behavioral difficulties may be addressed in a variety of ways. Some
teachers are trained in working with behavioral disordered children and
they know behavior modification and can use it in the regular classroom.
In other cases, the child is sent to a resource room for behavior modification and academic tutoring for part of the day. Still in other cases, the
child is placed in a self-contained classroom where he stays with one
teacher during the entire school day.

INTERVENTIONS FOR ADOLESCENTS

The adolescent with behavior disorders represents a rather severe
challenge for educators, mental health specialists, and family members.

Generally, this group of young people exhibits a variety of problems and the drop-out from school rate for these youngsters is over 40 percent. Of this number, about one-third are neither working nor involved in any type of vocational training. Some educators have suggested that as many as 40 percent of this drop-out population will be engaged in some type of criminal activity.

The young person who is chronically delinquent presents challenging problems for school personnel. These children, even when they go to school, do not pay attention to the instruction and seem completely bored and often hostile to the other children and the teachers. The self-contained classroom, along with vocational rehabilitation and special psychological therapy, is prescribed for this type child. The object is to change the behavior of the child to make him more accepted by society, and also train him in some areas so that when he leaves school he can get a job. It is possible that some of these youngsters will go on to college, but the majority of them should be trained in some type of skill whereby they can work when they leave school. If they are not trained in some type area where they can get a job, they often resort to robbery or other types of felonies which could land them in prison.

In summary, we have discussed children who have mild, moderate, or severe behavior disorders. Obviously, the ones with the severe behavior disorder are quickly recognized by other people in society. Children with mild behavior disorders often are not recognized by teachers and peers at school. The children with mild problems sometimes are not even recognized to have these problems by their parents. Children with moderate behavior problems stand out more than the ones with mild problems, but don't stand out like the ones with severe problems. There is a very large group of children with mild to moderate behavior problems who continue going to school, make adequate grades, and some go on and have very successful lives. The group of children with severe behavior problems are the group that give the school, parents, and society the most problems. These are the ones that we strive to help with behavior modification, job training, socialization training, any type of therapy that will help, and hope that as an adult this individual will have learned to use mechanisms which are acceptable to society in solving and coping with his problems.

REFERENCES

American Psychiatric Association. (1987). *Diagnostic and statistical manual of mental disorders* (3rd ed., rev.). Washington, DC: Author.

Bower, E. M. (1959). The emotionally handicapped child and the school. *Exceptional Children, 26,* 6–11.

Center for Social Policy. (1990). *Kids count data book.* Washington, DC: Author.

Children's Defense Fund. (1989). *A vision for America's future: An agenda for the 1990s.* Washington, DC: Author.

Council for Exceptional Children. (1991). *Report of the CEC advocacy and governmental relations committee regarding the new proposed U.S. federal definition of serious emotional disturbance.* Reston, VA: Author.

Forest, M., & Pearpoint, J. (1990). Supports for addressing severe maladaptive behavior. In W. Stainback & S. Stainback (Eds.), *Support networks for inclusive schooling: Interdependent integrated education.* Baltimore: Paul H. Brookes.

Forness, S. (1992). Broadening the cultural-organizational perspective in exclusion of youth with social maladjustment. *Remedial and Special Education, 13*(1), 55–59.

Forness, S., & Kavale, K. (1988). Psychopharmacologic treatment: A note on classroom effects. *Journal of Learning Disabilities, 32,* 48–55.

Forness, S. R., & Knitzer, J. K. (1990) *A new proposed definition and terminology to replace "serious emotional disturbance" in the Education of the Handicapped Act.* Alexandria, VA: National Mental Health Association.

Guetzloe, E. (1988). Suicide and depression: Special education's responsibility. *Teaching Exceptional Children,* 20(4), 24–28.

Hardman, M., Drew, C., Egan, W., & Wolf, B. (1993). *Human Exceptionality.* Boston: Allyn & Bacon.

Kirk, S., Gallagher, J., & Anastasiow, N. (1993). *Educating Exceptional Children.* Boston: Houghton Mifflin.

Knitzer, J. (1982). *Unclaimed children: The failure of public responsibility to children and adolescents in need of mental health services.* Washington, DC: Children's Defense Fund.

Paul, J., & Epanchin, B. (Eds.). (1986). *Emotional disturbance in children* (3rd ed.). Columbus, OH: Merrill.

Peacock Hill Working Group. (1990). *Problems and promises in special education and related services for children and youth with emotional and behavioral disorders.* Charlottesville, VA: Author.

Quay, H. C. (1975). Classification in the treatment of delinquency and antisocial behavior. In N. Hobbs (Ed.), *Issues in the classification of children* (Vol. 1). San Francisco: Jossey-Bass.

Quay, H. C. (1979). Classification. In H. C. Quay & J. S. Werry (Eds.), *Psychopathological disorders of childhood* (2nd ed.). New York: Wiley.

Quay, H., & Werry, J. (Eds.). (1986). *Psychological disorders in childhood* (3rd ed.). New York: Wiley.

Swartz, S. L., Mosley, W. J., & Koenig-Jerz, G. (1987, April). *Diagnosing behavior disorders: An analysis of eligibility criteria and recommended procedures.* Paper presented at the Annual Convention of the Council for Exceptional Children, Chicago, IL.

U.S. Department of Education. (1990). *Twelfth annual report to Congress on the implementation of the Education of the Handicapped Act.* Washington, DC: U.S. Department of Education.

Von Isser, A., Quay, H. C., & Love, C. T. (1980). Interrelationships among three measures of deviant behavior. *Exceptional Children, 46,* 272–276.

Wood, F. (1982). Defining disturbing, disordered, and disturbed behavior. In F. Wood & K. Laken (Eds.), *Disturbing, disoriented, or disturbed?* Reston, VA: Council for Exceptional Children.

Chapter 6

COMMUNICATION DISORDERS

One-fourth of the children (ages 6–21) with disabilities who were served under federal law during 1989–90 had speech or language impairments (U.S. Department of Education, 1991).

Deaf parents who have children who are deaf have noticed that their children appear to babble with their hands just as infants who hear babble through speech (Reuter News Agency, 1991).

Use the Fast Food Passport! Welcome to Wendy's! A customer having language or speech that is difficult to understand can flip to cards that have pictures of food thus indicating what he or she wants (Crestwood Company, 1987–88).

SPEECH AND LANGUAGE DISORDERS—WHAT ARE THEY?

Palmer and Yanks (1990) state that speech and language disorders are observed disturbances in the normal speech, language, or hearing process. Hedges (1991) tells us that disordered communication calls attention to itself, interferes with communication, and makes both the speaker and listener uncomfortable. IDEA defines the term speech and language impairment in this way:

Speech or language impairment means a communication disorder such as stuttering, impaired articulation, a language impairment, or a voice impairment that adversely affects a child's educational performance (C.F.R., Part 300, Section 300.7, 1992). The basic components of the communication process consists of the sender, the message and the receiver. Speech is the systematic production of words of a particular language. Kirk, Gallagher, and Anastasiow (1993) say that sounds become speech only if they are used to produce words which have meaning. They also tell us that speech has a rhythmic flow with stress and intonation and words with stressed and unstressed syllables. The following is a simple overview of the production of speech. There is a thought in the brain and it is translated into symbols and sent to the breathing areas for resonation and phonation. After that the air is sent to be modified by movements of the tongue and passage over the teeth and lips, which help to form the sounds, words, and sentences of a

114

particular language (articulation). When this thought is received by a listener we have audition.

Kirk, Gallagher, and Anastasiow (1993) list the following four components which are involved in the production of speech:

Respiration (breathing) is the process that generates and produces sound.
Phonation is the production of sound by the vibration of the vocal cords.
Resonation is the production of sound that gives the voice a unique characteristic and identifies the person. It is the product of sound traveling through the person's head and neck.
Articulation is the movement of the mouth and tongue that shapes sound into phonemes (the smallest unit of sound) that make speech (p. 265).

TYPICAL SPEECH DEVELOPMENT

Speech sounds are created as air passes through the vocal track (larynx, pharynx, mouth, and nose). We vary the position of the lips, tongue, and lower jaw in order to form the sounds.

In the first eight years of life, children must learn to produce all the consonants, vowels, and diphthongs which makeup the sounds of the English language. The child learns these sounds in a fairly consistent sequence, but there may be as much as a three-year variance between the time that some children learn a particular sound and the time that others learn the same sound (McCormick, 1990a).

Table 6.1
Typical ages for mastery of consonant sounds

By age 3:	/p/, /m/, /h/, /n/, /w/
By age 4:	/b/, /k/, /g/, /d/, /f/, /y/
By age 6:	/t/, /ng/, /r/, /l/, /s/
By age 7:	/ch/, /sh/, /j/, voiceless /th/
By age 8:	/s/, /z/, /v/, voiced /th/
Even later:	/zh/

Table 6.1 shows the typical age at which 90 percent of all children are able to produce the different consonant sounds.

Each person develops a voice that is as unique as fingerprints. Our voices are made up of a number of elements, but primarily include pitch, loudness, and resonance. Pitch is determined by the mass, tension, and elasticity of the vocal folds and the rate of vibration of the vocal folds.

The intensity of our voice is determined by the air pressure coming from the lungs through the vocal folds. In essence, intensity is a perception of the listener, but the loudness of the voice is controlled by the air pressure. Resonance is determined by the way we modify the tone coming from the vocal folds by using the cavities of the throat, mouth, and nose. Proctor (1989) tells us that the distinct sound of a newborn compared to the cry of an older infant is partially a result of growth and changes in these cavities during the first few months of life. And finally, the quality of the voice is a result of several factors which combine.

Robert. Robert was 55 years old when he was involved in an automobile accident. He suffered a head injury that did not appear to be serious. By the time he was released from the hospital (2 days later) Robert noticed that he was having trouble remembering things. Later he was diagnosed as suffering from aphasia.

A year after the accident, Robert has trouble speaking and he communicates through notes. Most of the time he understands what is said to him but at times he just looks blank at the person talking to him. He still has his job but communicates by writing notes; he has been told to consider early retirement. Robert is trying to relearn language through a rehabilitation program.

Alice. Alice is nine years old. Her mother and father are both well educated. Until the age of four, Alice exhibited normal language. However, at age four, her parents noticed she had a fluency problem with her language. She knows that if she says anything at breakfast to Mom or Dad she will stutter. She dreads seeing people. At school she knows the answers to the teacher's questions but will not raise her hand to be called on. She hates it when people finish the sentences that she is trying to say. "God, if I could just stay in bed every morning" she thinks. "I don't have any problems until I have to face people." She looks in the mirror and says to herself, "If I could just hide!"

Murphy and Moon (1993) state that infants at early ages differentiate these various features to recognize their mother's voices. Allen and Marotz (1989) say that by four to eight months of age, babies recognize the differences in voice quality that indicate anger, happiness, and sadness and can use their own voices to indicate satisfaction, happiness, and anger.

In our speech development, fluency becomes a part of us and this fluency should be easy, smooth, flowing, effortless speech.

Many children while learning to communicate have problems with fluency. They repeat words and sounds as they try to communicate and especially when they try to express ideas or concepts more advanced than their language or speech skills. Children "trip" as they talk just like they did in early life when they were learning to walk.

CHARACTERISTICS OF SPEECH IMPAIRMENTS

When a child is developing speech, he can have impairments in articulation, voice, or fluency. Students who have hearing losses or cerebral palsy often have articulation disorders or voice disorders. However, articulation, voice, or fluency disorders can be present as single disorders.

Articulation Disorders

Articulation disorders are by far the largest group of speech and language impairments. Hulit and Howard (1993) tell us that an articulation disorder occurs when the student is unable to produce the various sounds and sound combinations of language. A student is said to have an articulation disorder when skills are atypical for a certain age level.

Articulation disorders consist of substitutions, omissions, additions, and distortions. Substitutions and omissions are the most common articulation disorders we find in children. When a child uses substitutions, he replaces the appropriate phoneme, or sound, with one that is easier to make. Common substitutions are /w/ for /r/, as in woad for road, or /t/ for /c/, as in tat for cat. Omissions occur when a child leaves a phoneme out of a word. Table 6.2 indicates some of the common articulation errors.

Table 6.2.
Common articulation errors.

Type	Description	Example
Substitution	/th/ for /s/ or /z/	saw, zipper
	/f/ for /th/	thumb, bathtub, both
	/w/ for /r/	rabbit, ear, carrot
	/b/ for /v/	valentine
Omission	final sounds	He ha(s) a bi(g) ha(t).
	blended sounds	I want the b(l)ue one.
Addition	extra sounds	Cans are aluminum.

"Note. From *Born to Talk:* L. M. Hulit and M. R. Howard, 1993, Allyn and Bacon. Copyright 1993 by Allyn and Bacon. All rights reserved. Reprinted by permission."

A child might omit sounds from blends such as boo for blue, and from the ends of words.

Additions are simple sounds added to words. In distortions, the child modifies the standard production of the phoneme in some manner. The listener gets the idea that the sound is being produced, but the sound is different or distorted. Table 6.2 points out some common articulation errors that children who have articulation problems make.

Voice Disorders

Voice disorders affect the quality of the voice itself. There are four dimensions of the voice:

> quality (breathy or strident)
> resonance (nasal or denasal)
> pitch (high or low)
> intensity (loud or soft)

The quality of the voice is affected by problems of breath support or vocal-fold functioning. The child's most common voice disorder is the vocal nodules caused by yelling and other forms of vocal abuse. Vocal nodules, which often develop because the vocal mechanism is used incorrectly, are somewhat like little calluses that form on the vocal folds. These nodules do not allow the folds to vibrate properly and they cannot come together completely. Because the folds cannot vibrate properly, the sound of a child's voice changes. When these folds cannot come together, the child may not be able to make any sounds from the larynx. If the nodules become too large, the child might very well lose his voice altogether. There are times when this problem is remedied through therapy, but it can also require surgery and therapy. The therapy is designed to teach the student to talk in a way that is not abusive to the vocal folds.

The voice disorders that are related to resonance are characterized by hypernasality and hyponasality. Children with hypernasality sound as if they are speaking through their noses. Typically, the air for all sounds except /m/, /n/, and /ng/ is directed through the mouth. In hypernasality, however, air is allowed to pass through the nose on other sounds as well. As a result, /b/ sounds like /m/ and /d/ like /n/. In hyponasality, on the other hand, air cannot pass through the nose and comes out through the mouth. In this condition, /m/ sounds like /b/ and /n/ like /d/. Everyone with a nose stuffed up with a cold has experienced this temporary hyponasality.

Disorders of vocal pitch usually occur when children or individuals have voices that are too high or too low in pitch. Generally, this disorder is found in men who say their voices are too high. Some women also believe that their voices are too low, but we find that more men seek therapy for this condition than women.

In disorders of intensity or problems of loudness, we seldom find individuals who have voices that are too loud. More often, they seek help because their voices are too soft.

Fluency Disorders

The final group of speech disorders are disorders of fluency and we often refer to this as stuttering. Stuttering is an interruption of the forward flow of speech, therefore, it is a problem of speech fluency.

All children and all adults are dysfluent on occasion. Normal dysfluency becomes stuttering when the disruptions in speech are accompanied by awareness, anxiety, or compensatory behaviors. If a child prolongs or repeats most words in his sentences and if he is aware of it and concerned about these deficiencies, he is described as a stutterer. Although experts do not agree on the exact definition and description of stuttering, most of them do agree that a sign of struggle or tension must be present as a characteristic of stuttering.

Stuttering is probably the most widely recognized type of speech problem. This recognition and interest is somewhat paradoxical because stuttering occurs infrequently and has one of the lowest prevalence rates compared to other speech disorders. For example, articulation disorders occur in the United States much more often than do stuttering problems.

The common view of stuttering partly comes from the nature of behavior involved in the problem. We know that stuttering is a disturbance in the rhythm influencing speech. It may involve certain sounds, syllables, words or phrases, and the problem elements may differ from individual to individual. Such interruptions in the flow of speech are very evident to both the speaker and the listener. They are probably more disruptive to the communication act than any other type of speech disorder.

Parents often become unnecessarily concerned about stuttering as their children learn to talk. As already mentioned, most children exhibit some fluency problems as they develop speech. Parents should not be concerned unless this problem persists. Parents will notice if there is blocking, repetition, and prolonging of sounds, syllables, words, or phrases. Parents will also notice if these diminish or if they become worse. If the stuttering problem continues, then of course the parents should seek the help of a therapist.

Causation of Stuttering. People have been searching for the cause of stuttering and it has lead behavioral scientists in many directions. One difficulty with the efforts has been that the researchers often have sought a single cause. The current thinking has suggested that stuttering probably has a variety of causes and the search for a single cause has been mostly discarded. Theories regarding causes of stuttering seem to take three basic approaches: (1) theories related to emotional problems, (2) theories that view stuttering as a result of a person's biological makeup or some neurological problem, and (3) theories that view stuttering as a learned behavior.

Many professionals have become less interested here of late in both the emotional and biological causation theories of stuttering. The emotional problem theory tends to be held predominantly by psychiatrists and certain counsellors. Van Riper and Emerick (1990) tell us that this may be because the stuttering clients they see in their clinical practice tend to have severe emotional problems. Research in this area is scarce and the topic is difficult to study because we have so few stutterers and because we don't know if the stuttering causes the emotional problems or if the emotional problems cause the stuttering.

There have been a few studies in the past years on the biological cause theory of stuttering. There is some research that has indicated that the brains of people who stutter may be organized differently than those who don't stutter, but the nature of such differences remains unclear at this time. Certain results have suggested that individuals who stutter when compared with those who don't stutter use different sections of the brain to process material.

A persistent theory over the years regarding the causation of stuttering has related to learning. This line of reasoning has viewed stuttering as a learned behavior that comes about during the early speech development. Most young children exhibit nonfluent speech as they develop communication skills. But from a learning view and if they are exposed to stutterers in the family, they may learn to stutter.

There has been some interest in the influence of heredity on stuttering. This issue has been approached for many years, but there is no concrete proof that stuttering is inherited. Because males who stutter outnumber females by four to one, it has been suggested that maybe the genetic material that determines gender may also carry material that contributes to stuttering. This hypothesis is difficult to test and remains only speculation. Heredity has also been of interest because of the high incidence of stuttering within certain families as well as with twins.

Interventions. Over the years, there have been many treatment approaches concerning people who stutter, but the results have been mixed. Therapists have used techniques such as play therapy, creative dramatics, parental counseling, group counseling with parents, and group counseling with parents and children. Even hypnosis has been used to treat some cases of stuttering, the success of hypnosis has been quite limited. Speech rhythm has been the focus of some therapy for stuttering. In some cases, this approach has included the use of a metronome to establish a rhythm for speaking. Relaxation therapy and biofeedback have also been used in trying to alleviate the symptoms of stuttering. In all of the techniques noted, the outcomes have become somewhat mixed and most authorities will tell us that there is no cure for stuttering.

DELAYED SPEECH

Delayed speech refers to a deficit in communication ability when a child speaks like someone who is much younger. If we take this from a developmental point of view, this type of difficulty involves a delayed beginning of speech and language. Very young children are generally able to communicate to some degree even before they have verbal behavior. The children use gestures, facial expressions, and other physical movements and vocalizations that would not be considered speech, such as grunts or squeals or nods of the head. This early development tells us that there is a relationship between communication, language, and speech.

It is difficult to distinguish among the three functions at this stage, so we are only concerned here with speech delay. Delayed speech is considered a failure of speech to develop at the expected age and along with other maturation delays such as crawling or sitting up or walking. We know that delayed speech is related to hearing impairment, mental retardation, emotional disturbance, and brain injury.

Children who have delayed speech often have few or no verbalizations that can be interpreted as conventional speech. Some of their communication is strictly through physical gestures. Perhaps they will use only a single word and will say "ball" instead of "Give me my ball." Or they may say 'want' instead of "I would like to have some milk." Some children may even beat their chests and grunt when they want to go to the bathroom.

The current prevalence of delayed speech is not clear, but the federal government did provide some estimates during 1989 and 1990 (U.S. Department of Education, 1991). For children with normal hearing, the instance of delayed speech is as low as 2 percent of the population.

Van Riper and Emerick (1990) indicate to us that the differences between stuttering and delayed speech are obvious. They go on to state that the distinctions between delayed speech and articulation disorders are not very clear. In fact, they say children with delayed speech usually make many articulation errors in their speech patterns. However, their major problems lie in grammatical and vocabulary deficits, which are more matters of developmental delay.

Causation. Cases having delayed speech often take a variety of forms so it is not surprising that the causes of these forms vary greatly. Several types of environmental deprivation contribute to delayed speech. A complete or partial hearing loss could cause an individual a serious delay or even absence of speech development. If the auditory stimulus in modeling are deficient, learning to speak will be extremely difficult. For those children with normal hearing, the environment may be a factor in delayed speech. In some homes, the child has little opportunity to learn speech. This happens in families where there is minimal conversation or in a family that does not allow the child to speak very often. There are other causes of delayed speech, of course, and some of these are cerebral palsy, emotional disturbance, mental retardation, autism, and negativism.

Negativism involves a conflict between parents' expectations and the child's ability to perform. A great deal of pressure is placed on this type of child during the period when he or she is normally developing speaking skills. They can't seem to do anything properly and the parents are constantly on them. In other words, the demands are great and these demands may exceed a child's performance and ability. Normally, when these children are developing their speaking skills, they are told to go to bed, they are told to control urination, they are told to go to the bathroom at certain times, they are told how to eat and what to eat, and as already stated, the demands are great. The child finds out that refusal is one way that he can get attention. He simply may not talk and he seems to withdraw from the family and remains silent. This creates commotions some times within the family and he gets a lot of attention, but at the same time, normal speech development is not taking place. Delayed speech may occur in extreme cases where negativism related to talking is prolonged.

INTERACTING WITH THE FAMILY— EARLY CHILDHOOD YEARS

Tips for the Family

If we are to model the speech and language of our infants after us, then we must talk to them in normal tones from a very early age even though he or she may not be communicating at that time. Parents should respond to babbling and other noises that the young child makes with conversations and ways to reinforce early verbal output. Parents should not overreact if the child is not developing at the same rate as someone else's infant because there are great variations between children. If parents are concerned about their child's speech development, they can have the child tested to determine if everything is going correctly. The parents should observe the early areas of development to assure themselves that the child is progressing in all areas of development. If parents are seeking a day care or a preschool program for their young child, they should search carefully for one which will provide a rich, systematic communication environment.

Tips for the Preschool Teacher

The preschool teacher should encourage parental involvement in all dimensions of her program and this includes systematic speech and language stimulation at home. The preschool teacher should also use all situations and events as opportunities to teach speech and language and to focus initially on concrete objects and later move to abstract objects, better helping the child to learn different words. A preschool teacher should also use the words what, who, when, and so on every time that the child starts a conversation. This gives the child many opportunities to practice speaking as well as to practice thinking. The preschool teacher should practice with the child the use of prepositions such as in, on, out, and so on. The preschool teacher should use all occasions possible to increase the child's vocabulary.

As the child grows and matures, there are other tips for the family during the child's elementary years and secondary/transition years. Tips for the family for the elementary years are shown in Table 6.3 and tips for the family during the secondary/transition years are shown in Table 6.4.

Table 6.3
Elementary Years—Tips for the Family

ELEMENTARY YEARS

Tips for the Family
  - Stay involved in your child's educational program through active participation with the school.
  - Work in collaboration with the child's teacher on speaking practice, blending it naturally into family and individual activities.
  - Communicate naturally with the child; avoiding "talk down" and thereby modeling the use of more simple language.
 	
Tips for the Regular Classroom Teacher
  - Continue promoting parental involvement in their child's intervention program in whatever manner they can participate.
  - Encourage the child with communication disorders to talk about events and things in his or her environment, describing experiences in as much detail as possible.
  - Use all situations possible to provide practice for the child's development of speech and language skills.
  - Continue to promote the enhancement of vocabulary for the child in a broad array of topic areas.
 	
Tips for School Personnel
  - Promote an environment where all who are available and in contact with the child are involved in communication instruction, if not directly then indirectly through interaction and modeling.
  - Begin encouraging student involvement in a wide array of activities that can also be used to promote speech and language development.
 	
Tips for Neighbors and Friends
  - Interact with children with communication disorders normally, not focusing on the speaking difficulties that may be evident.
  - As a neighbor or friend, provide support for the child's parents, who may be struggling with difficult feelings about the child's communication skills.

DISORDERS OF LANGUAGE

It has already been mentioned that the elements of language are governed by culturally determined rules of correct usage. Each of the elements—phonology, morphology, syntax, pracmatics, and semantics—is a potential source of language disorder. It is difficult for some children to express age appropriate ideas in correct sentence structures, with verb tenses, or with the use of prefixes, and suffixes.

Language involves both reception and expression and in some manner

Table 6.4
Secondary/Transition Years—Tips for the Family

SECONDARY/TRANSITION YEARS
Tips for the Family - Children who still exhibit communication problems at this level are likely to perform on a lower level, suggesting that communication may focus on functional matters such as grooming, feeding, and so on. - For some children, communication may involve limited verbalization, and consideration should be given to other means of interacting. - To the degree possible, continue to interact with your child as much and as normallly as possible. **Tips for the Regular Classsroom Teacher** - Communication instruction should be embedded in the context of functional areas (e.g., social interactions, request for assistance, choice making. - Augmented communication devices or procedures may be added to the student's curriculum. **Tips for School Personnel** - Encourage the development of school activities that will encourage use of a broad variety of skill levels in speaking (i.e., not just the debate club). - Promote the development of school activities that permit participation through alternative communication modes other than speaking. **Tips for Neighbors and Friends** - To the degree that you are comfortable, interact with children with communication disorders using alternative communication approaches (e.g., signs, gesturing, pantomiming).

it is probably processed internally during both reception and expression. Processing errors interfere with all types of learning and this includes language learning.

The stages and sequences of normal language acquisition gives clues to language disorders. It is very difficult to determine a specific cause for a specific language disorder for an individual child. Also, speech problems, developmental disorders, or other disabilities may influence a child's ability to use language.

In summary, any deviation from linguistic competence involves the following and should be considered (see Table 6.5).

Table 6.5
Disorders of Language

```
1.  Producing understandable sounds (articulation and
    pronunciation)
2.  Creating well-formed sentences and understanding
    grammatical structures (syntax and morphology)
3.  Creating sentences with meaningful content (semantics)
4.  Constructing logical sentences with appropriate knowledge
    (for example, saying "I see a bird," when the child
    actually sees a bird, nor an airplane)
5.  Speaking appropriately in context (pragmatics)

    Linguistic competence also involves:

1.  Receptive understanding (hearing and cognition)
2.  Expressive communication (cognition and speaking)
3.  Cognitive understanding (intelligence)
4.  Interactive skills (self-confidence and social
    orientation)
5.  Physical and motor skills (facial expressions, supportive
    gestures, and uses of throat, tongue, and lips)
```

PEER LINGUISTIC DIVERSITY

As already stated, children learn to speak the language spoken in their homes and neighborhoods. Children tend to use language to express their needs and thoughts in the ways that their parents do. In some homes, parents use language in ways that are different from the language some teachers expect students to use. For example, teachers may demand explicitness in language, whereas children do not demonstrate explicitness in language. A child may use two words to indicate a sentence when actually the sentence should have seven or eight words. The child has learned to use just two words at home and the teacher expects the child to use seven or eight words in class. This calls for confrontation.

Teachers should be aware that differences in language usage such as this should not be treated as deficits. They can be addressed by teaching and not by therapy.

ASSESSMENT OF NON-ENGLISH-SPEAKING CHILDREN

When children come from homes in which English is not the primary language, then they are going to have difficulty in using English in school. Language differences can and should be identified early, and language skills should be taught to avoid failure. All children should be tested in their language so that we will know their strengths and weaknesses, not only on IQ tests, but on achievements tests as well.

Children from communities that speak a language other than American English need assessments by a speech-language pathologist who is skilled in the child's primary language. Services for these children are mandated in Parts B and H of Section 16 of the Individuals with Disabilities Education Act of 1990.

Children who are bilingual naturally vary in their English competence. Some speak only a few words of English, but others speak English fairly well. Any assessment of these children should involve a specialist who is bicultural and bilingual and one who speaks American English and the language in the homes of the children being tested.

Great care must be taken that children from different cultures who speak a different language are assessed by a person skilled in the child's language and cultural mores. If this is not done, we will label a child as mentally retarded or one can be labeled as illiterate when actually the child is above average in intelligence and has above average skills in academics.

Another issue is that the child may not understand American English and he may also not understand the Mexican-American Spanish that is spoken in the classroom. The child may speak a type of Spanish that is not the Mexican-American Spanish spoken in the classroom. For example, he may speak Puerto Rican English. He may not also understand the dialect of the Mexican-American Spanish, but he can understand the dialect of the Puerto Rican Spanish. The assessor must be from the same Spanish-speaking subgroup of the child. It is very easy to label a child retarded or one who is functioning below average in academics by a person who does not speak the child's language or the particular dialect that the child speaks.

DIALECTS

There is a wide variation in word usage or pronunciation in our society. Where a child lives will influence the child's use of language. Dialects are ways of pronouncing language within geographic regions where the language use may differ from the literary form. For example, in certain parts of Arkansas people say "warsh" for "wash" and this is not a speech defect, but a regional dialect. However, if a child says dog for cow, then that is a deficit.

A dialect is very much a part of a child's language and self-concept and must be dealt with carefully by people. Teachers need to model correct forms and encourage correct form of the English language, but they should allow the use of the dialect in informal speech if communication is clear.

IDENTIFICATION AND ASSESSMENT

Preschool Children and Early Intervention

Much of language development begins before a child says his first word. Most of the tests for language delays or problems, however, are not administered until the child is two years or older. The criterion that is often used for administering diagnostic tests is the failure of the child to know fifty words by the age of two years. If the child has mastered fewer than fifty words by two, it may indicate that a communication problem exists.

Kirk, Gallagher, and Anastasiow (1993) tell us that in many school systems, four general procedures are involved in identifying children who have communication disorders.

1. Screening children who are suspected of having communication disorders and who may need additional testing or a full evaluation.
2. Evaluating those identified during screening and from referrals with appropriate speech and language assessment tools.
3. Diagnosing the type and severity of communication disorders according to the criteria of the evaluation data.
4. Making appropriate placement decisions for those children who need speech or language intervention and developing an IEP or IFEP for them (p. 284).

Screening

Most school systems have established formal screening programs for vision, hearing, and communication problems. Parents or teachers often request that a child be screened. Speech/language pathologists often conduct screening in selected grades at the beginning of the school year and this is done to identify those children suspected of having disorders of articulation, fluency, voice, or language. Screening is sometimes a yes/no process. By this, the author means that if the child does need further evaluation, this is a yes; or no, this child does not need further evaluation at this time. If in doubt, an assessment is usually conducted by the speech/language pathologist. The purpose of rapid screening is (1) detection and (2) planning for fast and accurate therapy.

Federal regulations do not require a parent's permission before a child participates in group screening; however, some school districts in some states require that parents be notified. Children who are identified through screening are then evaluated more thoroughly.

Evaluation and Diagnosis

After we evaluate children suspected of having communication problems, we usually follow the process with the following steps:

Obtaining Parental Permission. Federal law requires that parents or the legally designated caregivers give permission before a child can be formally tested for communication disorders or any other disorder.

Taking a Case History. This is required by public law and the speech pathologist often takes the case history from the child and from the parents of the child. This history often includes background information about the child's development, a health history, family information, social history, school achievement records, and if there are other evaluations, data from those.

Assessing the Disorder. The speech pathologist clinician assesses the type and the severity of the disorder using formal speech and language tests. The clinician may also use informal procedures such as language sampling and analysis of the child's conversation. The clinician also evaluates the structure and function of the speech mechanism.

Assessing Other Areas. The speech clinician may be interested in the other areas which have been assessed by a psychologist or from teachers. The speech clinician requests the child's folder and can read the reports about intelligence testing and educational assessment. Often physical therapists or occupational therapists are involved and the speech clinician ought to read their reports also.

Making a Diagnosis. The speech pathologist will talk to the other professionals and then make a diagnosis of the child's speech problems.

Developing the Individualized Education Program. The speech/language clinician may lead the school team in developing an IEP for the child with a communication disorder. The child's teacher, though, will lead the team in developing an IEP for the child's academic placement. Parental permission is required for the plan to be implemented. Intervention for the communication disorder outlined in the IEP generally is based on all the assessment data, the diagnosis, and other characteristics about the child, such as his IQ and certain learning deficits that he may have.

Educational Adaptations. Language, speech, and hearing services often are offered by speech/language pathologists in a variety of settings: schools, clinics, hospitals, university speech clinics, and private offices. Professionals who help children with communication disorders often are a part of a clinical team that provides many services which supplement the regular school program.

The speech/language pathologist often has a case load of 150 students: therefore, work on the IEP is limited and the speech/language pathologist often does not have time to give children in the school setting all the help they need. There are some schools where the speech/language pathologist will have only 50 cases and this person can help more readily in the diagnosis, IEP, and every phase of the child's speech/language program.

Mainstreaming is an important option for the child with communication disorders. Children generally stay in the regular classroom until it is time for speech therapy. The child then goes to the resource room where the speech/language pathologist is located and has speech therapy in that resource room. After the speech therapy is concluded, the child will go back to the regular classroom and finish the rest of the day unless he has other special education services which are required and then he will go back to the resource room.

Intervention Strategies

Therapy. The speech/language pathologist knows each child and brings to each therapy session a large amount of knowledge and a set of skills to recognize and remediate each child's specific problem. The kind of therapy required for each child will depend upon the child's assessment. The most common kind of therapeutic procedure for most young children is play therapy. This is sometimes called role playing. Play, as has been mentioned, is a way children without disabilities learn speech and language. In the therapy sessions, therapists model the way nondisabled children learn language. The child with a language problem uses the speech therapist as a model to try to adjust his own language.

TYPICAL LANGUAGE DEVELOPMENT

The author would like to end this chapter by going through various stages of language development from birth to six years. If a teacher knows the phases that a child goes through, then the teacher can observe any deficits that a child has when he is not going through these stages. It is also important for a parent to know the stages that a child goes through. From birth to six months, the child will cry when he has certain emotions and he will also cry when he is hungry and feels pain. During this time, the child coos in response to familiar situations and he also laughs. From birth to six months, the child will respond to voices and other sounds differently.

From six to 12 months, the child will listen to new words and he will understand his own name and the word "No." The child will use many sounds differentially and with inflection. He will also babble. The child will imitate sound patterns and motor acts such as waving good-bye. He will respond to simple commands, "come here" or "give me." The child during this time will recognize the name of familiar people.

From 12 to 18 months, the child will name familiar objects with a single word. He will mix jargon which is speech sounds with inflection with single words. The child will use speech socially to interact with others and he will recognize words and commands. During this period, the child will have from five- to 50-word vocabulary and he will be able to identify one to three body parts. That is at 18 months, and he can answer such questions as, "Where is your nose?", "Point to a book," and "I am pointing to my _____."

From 18 to 24 months, the child can string two or more words together. This child will have a 2- to 300-word vocabulary by 24 months and he will also understand possessives. During this time, the child will use plurals, and he no longer uses jargon by the age of 24 months. During this time, the child also uses simple adverbs and adjectives such as big, nice, good, and he also uses some verbs. He understands and he often ignores simple directives. The child also, during this time, will listen to his parents speech and imitate important parts of it.

During the 24- to 36-month period, the child will understand objects by use such as, "What do we eat with?" and "What do we eat on?" The child will understand simple questions and pronouns and he understands the prepositions, in, on, under, up, and down. This child can follow two-step directions and he also will listen to stories. He will take turns in communicating with others and he will use two word and longer phrases. By this time, the child should have a vocabulary between 900 and 1,000 words. The child can recount events and ask simple questions during this period.

During the period of 36 to 48 months, the child will ask certain questions, who, what, when, where, and how, and he will tell stories, both real and imaginary. During this time the child will understand compound and complex sentences, and he will use some. He will be able to explain and describe events and will have a vocabulary of 1,000 to 1,500 words. The child will ask questions and he will use communication to talk with his play mates.

Between the ages of four and five years, the child will use prepositions in, on, and under and he will understand if, because, why, and when. This child will use conjunctions and longer, more complex sentences. During this time, the child will still make some grammatical errors, but he can give first and last names, gender, and his telephone number. He also uses the past tense.

During the five- to six-year period, the child will have a vocabulary of 2,500 to 2,800 words. The child will respond to most complex sentences and sometimes he will be confused. He will use comparative adjectives such as big, bigger, biggest and he will use irregular verbs such as be, go, swim. The child will correctly use a and the during this period. Also during this period, the child will tell familiar stories and imaginative tales and he will share personal feelings and thoughts verbally. He will talk things out rather than always act them out and he can use a telephone and he can recognize and tell jokes.

REFERENCES

Allen, K. E. & Marotz, L. (1989). *Developmental profiles: Birth to six.* Albany, NY: Delmar.

Crestwood Company. (1987–1988). *Communications aids for children and adults* (Catalog). Milwaukee, WI: Author.

Hardman, M., Drew, C., Egan, W., & Wolf, B. (1993). *Human Exceptionality* (4th ed.). Boston: Allyn and Bacon.

Hedges, M. N. (1991). *Introduction to communicative disorders.* Austin, TX: PRO-ED.

Kirk, S., Gallagher, J., & Anastasiow, N. (1993). *Educating Exceptional Children* (7th ed.). Boston: Houghton Mifflin.

Palmer, J. M., & Yantis, P. A. (1990). *Survey of communication disorders.* Baltimore: Williams & Wilkins.

McCormick, L. (1990a). Sequence of language and communication development. In L. McCormick & R. Schiefelbusch (Eds.), *Early language intervention: An introduction* (pp. 71–108). New York: Merrill/Macmillan.

Proctor, A. (1989). Stages of normal non-cry vocal development in infancy: A protocol for assessment. *Topics in Language Disorders, 10*(1), 26–42.

Reuter News Agency. (1991, March 25). *Babbling with hands by deaf babies casts doubt on speech-language tie.* Salt Lake Tribune, p. A1.

Sander, E. (1972). When are speech sounds learned? *Journal of Speech and Hearing Disorders, 37,* 55–63.

U.S. Department of Education (1991). To assure the free appropriate public education of all children with disabilities. *Thirteenth annual report to Congress on the implementation of the Individual with Disabilities Act.* Washington, DC: Author.

Van Riper, C., & Emerick, L. (1990). *Speech correction: An introduction to speech pathology and audiology* (8th ed.). Englewood Cliffs, NJ: Prentice Hall.

Chapter 7

MILD HEARING IMPAIRMENTS

> No deaf child who has earnestly tried to speak the words which he has never heard—to come out of the prison of silence, where no tone of love, no song of bird, no strain of music ever pierces the stillness—can forget the thrill of surprise, the joy of discovery which came over him when he uttered his first word. Only such a one can appreciate the eagerness with which I talked to my toys, to stones, trees, birds, and dumb animals, or the delight I felt when at my call Mildred ran to me or my dogs obeyed my commands. It is an unspeakable boon to me to be able to speak in winged words that need no interpretation.
>
> *The Story of My Life,* Helen Keller

Hearing impairment is a detriment to learning to speak even when the child is hearing impaired and not severe enough to be classified as deaf. There are many classifications of hearing impairments. Educators are concerned with how much the hearing loss affects the child's ability to speak and acquire language. The following definition reflects the educational orientation:

- *Hearing impairment:* A generic term indicating a hearing disability which may range in severity from mild to profound: it includes the subsets of *deaf* and *hard of hearing.*
- A *deaf* person is one whose hearing disability precludes successful processing of linguistic information through audition, with or without a hearing aid.
- A *hard of hearing* person is one who, generally with the use of a hearing aid, has residual hearing sufficient to enable successful processing of linguistic information through audition (Brill, MacNeil, & Newman, 1986, p. 67)

Educators are concerned about the age of onset. For this reason professionals working with the deaf use the terms congenitally deaf (those who were born deaf) and adventitiously deaf (those who acquire deafness after birth). Some professionals use *prelingual deafness* meaning "deafness present at birth or occurring early in life prior to the development of language." *Postlingual deafness* is "deafness occurring at any age

134

following the development of speech and language" (Brill, MacNeil, & Newman, 1986, p. 67).

There are many myths surrounding the subject of deaf and hearing impaired children and adults. Table 7.1 presents many myths we hold about the hearing impaired and the facts as we presently know them.

A hearing impairment is defined according to the degree of hearing loss. This is accomplished by testing a person's sensibility to sound intensity (loudness) and pitch (sound frequency). The unit we use to measure sound intensity is called the decibel (db), and the range of human hearing is approximately 0 to 130 db. Sounds above 130 db are very painful for the human. Table 7.2 demonstrates various sounds we might hear and their measured decibal levels.

THE HEARING PROCESS

Audition is defined as the act or sense of hearing. The auditory process involves the transmission of sound through the vibration of an object to a receiver. This process originates with the vibrator, such as a membrane, that causes displacement of air particles. In order for a vibration to become a sound, there must be a medium to carry it. The most common carrier is air, but vibrations can also be carried by metal, by water, and other substances. The displacement of air particles by the vibrator produces a pattern of circular waves that move away from the source.

We refer to this movement as a sound wave and if you can imagine the ripples which result from a pebble that is dropped in a pool of water, then that is the way it is. Sound waves are patterns of pressure that alternately push together and then pull apart in a spherical expansion. These sound waves are carried through the medium of air to a receiver. The human ear is a very sensitive receiver and is capable of being activated by incredibly small amounts of pressure. If we consider the small size of the ear, we then know that it is a prodigious instrument. With equipment that could almost be packaged in a small tube of sugar, the human can distinguish all of the sounds of speech and approximately a half a million other sounds.

The ear is a mechanism through which sound is collected, processed, and transmitted to a part of the brain that then decodes sensations into meaningful language.

Table 7.1
Myths and Facts about Persons with Hearing Impairment

Myth	Fact
Deafness leads automatically to inability to speak.	Even though hearing impairment, especially with greater degrees of hearing loss, is a barrier to normal development, some deaf people can be taught some understanding of oral language and the ability to speak.
Deafness is not as great a handicap as blindness.	Although it is impossible to predict the exact consequences of a handicap on a person's functioning, in general deafness is a greater handicap than blindness. This is due to a large degree to the effects hearing loss can have on the ability to understand and speak oral language.
The deaf child is inherently lower in intellectual ability.	It is generally believed that unless they are born with additional handicaps, deaf infants have the same intellectual capacities as hearing infants. Deaf individuals, however, may perform more poorly on some tasks because of their difficulty in communicating with those who hear.
In learning to understand what is being said to them, deaf individuals concentrate on reading lips.	*Lipreading* refers only to visual cues arising from movement of the lips. Some deaf people not only learn to lipread but also learn to make use of a variety of other visual cues, such as facial expressions and movements of the jaw and tongue. They thus engage in what is referred to as *speechreading*, a term that covers all visual cues associated with speaking.
Teaching American Sign Language is harmful to a child and may hamper development of oral language.	Most authorities today recognize the value of American Sign Language as a means of communication.
American Sign Language is a loosely structured group of gestures.	American Sign Language is a true language in its own right with its own set of grammatical rules.
American Sign Language can only be used to convey concrete ideas.	American Sign Language can be used at any level of abstraction.

"Note. From *Exceptional Children* (Sixth Ed.), by D. P. Hallahan and J. M. Kaufman, 1991, Allyn and Bacon. Copyright 1991 by Allyn and Bacon. Adapted by permission."

THE EXTERNAL EAR

The outer ear is made up of cartilage and is on the side of the head and we call it the auricle or pinna, and an external ear canal which was

Table 7.2
Estimated Decible (db) Levels of Common Environmental Sounds

Decibel Level (sound Intensity)	Source of Sound
140 db	Jet aircraft (75 feet from tail to takeoff)
130 db	Jackhammer
120 db	Thunder
110 db	Rock concert
100 db	Chain saw
90 db	Street traffic
80 db	Telephone ringing
70 db	Door Slam
60 db	Washing Machine
50 db	Conversational Speech
40 db	Electric Typewriter
30 db	Pencil Writing
20 db	Watch Ticking
10 db	Whisper
0 db	Lowest threshold of hearing for the human ear

referred to as the meatus. The auricle is the only outwardly visible part of the ear and is attached to the skull by three ligaments. The purpose of the auricle is to collect sound waves and then funnel those sound waves into the meatus. The meatus secretes wax which we call cerumen, which protects the inner structures of the ear by trapping foreign materials and it also lubricates the canal and eardrum. We call the eardrum the tempanic membrane and it is located at the inner end of the canal between the external and middle ear. The concave membrane is positioned in such a manner that when struck by sound waves, it vibrates freely.

THE MIDDLE EAR

The inner surface of the eardrum is located in the air-filled cavity of the middle ear. This surface consists of three small bones which we call the ossicular chain. These three bones are the malleus, incus, and stapes, and we often refer to them as the hammer, anvil, and stirrup. These three bones transmit the vibrations from the external ear through the cavity of the middle ear to the inner ear.

The eustachian tube is a structure that extends from the throat to the middle-ear cavity. The purpose of this tube is to equalize the air pressure in the eardrum with that of the outside air pressure. This is accomplished by controlling the flow of air into the middle-ear cavity. Though air conduction is the primary avenue through which sound reaches the inner ear, it is possible for conduction to occur through the bones of the skull. Bone conduction appears comparable to air conduction in that the patterns of displacement produced in the inner ear are similar.

THE INNER EAR

This part of the ear consists of a multitude of intricate passage ways. The cochlea lies horizontally in front of the vestibule which is a central cavity where sound enters directly from the middle ear. The sound waves are activated by movement in the ossicular chain. The cochlea is filled with fluid similar in composition to cerebral spinal fluid. Within the cochlea is corti's organ, a structure of highly specialized cells that translate vibrations into nerve impulses that are sent directly to the brain.

The other major structure within the inner ear is called the vestibular mechanism. This mechanism contains the semicircular canals that control balance. The semicircular canals have enlarged portions at one end and are filled with fluid that responds to head movement. The vestibular mechanism integrates sensory input which passes into the brain and assists the body in maintaining equilibrium. Motion and gravity are detected through this mechanism which allows the individual to differentiate between sensory input and body movement and from that of the external environment. Whenever the basic function of the vestibular mechanism or any other structures in the external, middle, and inner ear are interrupted, hearing loss may occur.

DEAF AND HARD OF HEARING

Deaf is a term that is commonly applied to describe a wide variety of hearing impairments. Deaf describes specifically those individuals whose hearing impairment is in the extreme range of loss—90 db or greater. Even if a human uses a hearing aid or other forms of amplification, the individual's primary means for developing language and communication is through the visual canal if he is deaf.

For a person who is hard of hearing, audition is deficient but remains somewhat functional. The person who is hard of hearing can generally use a hearing aid and he has residual hearing which is sufficient to enable successful processing of linguistic information through hearing.

The distinction between deaf and hard of hearing is not as clear as many traditional definitions imply.

TYPES OF HEARING LOSS

Conductive Hearing Losses

A conductive hearing loss reduces the intensity of sound reaching the inner ear where the auditory nerves begin. Sound waves must pass through the ear canal, as already stated, to the *tempanic membrane.* When something interferes with the intensity of sound before it gets to the tempanic membrane or before reaching the auditory nerve, there is a loss in conduction. The sequence of vibrations can be held up any where from the external to the inner ear. Wax or a malformation can block the external canal, the ear drum can be broken or punctured, or the movement of the bones in the middle can be obstructed. Conductive defects seldom cause losses more than 60 to 70 db.

Sensorineural Hearing Losses

Sensorineural hearing losses are caused by defects of the inner ear (cochlea) or the auditory nerve, particularly the delicate sensory hairs of the inner ear or the nerves that supply them, as these transmit impulses to the brain. Sensorineural hearing losses can affect only certain frequencies and these are the high ones.

Mixed Hearing Losses

Mixed hearing losses are those in which problems occur in the outer ear as well as middle or inner ear. Thus, these persons may hear distorted sounds as well as have difficulty with sound level.

Central Hearing Losses

Central hearing losses are hearing losses resulting from changes in the reception of hearing areas in the brain or damage to the pathways of the brain.

MEANS OF TESTING HEARING LOSS

Pure Tone Audiometry

Pure Tone Audiometry, which is the most common means of determining hearing loss, can be applied in children about three years of age and older. The audiometer, which is an instrument for testing hearing acuity, presents pure tones to the individual who receives the tones through a headset. The audiometer presents a range of sounds and measures the frequency and intensity that the individual is able to hear through the earphones. The individual being tested responds to the sounds by raising his or her hand to indicate if he can hear the tone. These responses are recorded on a graph called an audiogram. From the examination results, the degree and range of hearing impairment can be determined.

Bone Conductor Test

With infants and preschool children younger than the age of three, it is common to use both a pure tone test and a bone conductor test which measures the movement of sound through the hearing system to the brain. The vibrations are received by electrodes placed on the child's ear. The reception of sound in the brain is recorded on a graph that charts the brain's response to the vibrations. These vibrations are put on a chart and the audiologist can tell what type of hearing losses that a youngster may have.

Behavioral Observation Audiometry

Behavioral Observation Audiometry is used to test hearing in children younger than three years of age. The parents place the child in an environment with attractive toys and watch his or her reactions as sounds are introduced in the room by an outsider. If the child does not turn his head, blink his eye, or make smiles or movements toward the sound, then a lack of response indicates that he may have a hearing problem.

Play Audiometry

Play Audiometry tests are conducted in a pleasant environment with toys that move and make sounds. These toys are used to illicit responses from the youngsters such as eye blinks and changes in respiration or heartbeat.

THE SCHOOL'S ROLE IN IDENTIFICATION

Children with mild to moderate hearing impairments are difficult to identify in public held screenings, but the school can help by watching for certain things. Children with mild or moderate hearing impairments often go undiagnosed until academic performance indicates a problem. A child who stares blankly at the teacher may not be hearing what the teacher is saying; also the child may be blocking out communication because he or she is emotionally disturbed.

The Classroom Teacher's Role

We often ask ourselves, how can a classroom teacher identify a child with a hearing loss so that he can be referred for a more comprehensive examination? The following things should be noted by the teacher as being suspect of a hearing disability:

1. Does a child appear to have a physical problem associated with his or her ears?
2. Does the child articulate sounds poorly, and particularly omit consonant sounds?
3. When listening to radio, television, or records, does the student turn the volume up so high that others complain?
4. Does the student cock the head or turn toward the speaker in an apparent effort to hear better?
5. Does the student frequently request that what has been said be repeated?
6. Is the student unresponsive or unattentive when spoken to in a normal voice?
7. Is the student reluctant to participate in oral activities?

CAUSES OF HEARING LOSS

The causes of hearing impairments are divided between the generic and the incidental. Each accounts for approximately 50 percent of the causes. Table 7.3 lists some common causes of hearing impairments. The reader should note the number of illnesses, infections, or accidents that can lead to hearing impairments after birth.

Genetic Causes of Hearing Loss

The genetic causes are due to disorders which are inherited from one or both of the parents. More than 200 different types of genetic deafness have been identified and can be inherited either from having a hearing parent or a nonhearing parent.

Children may have other genetic defects which are associated with hearing defects. For example, children with Down syndrome have nar-

Table 7.3
Some Causes and Conditions Associated with
Hearing Impairments in School-age Children

Conductive Hearing Impairment	
Ottis media (including middle ear fluid)	Perforation of the tympanic membrane
Ottis externa	Impacted cerumen (wax)
Discontinuity of the ossicles	Blockage of the external auditory meatus by foreign object
Congenital malformation of the outer ear	Cholesteatoma
Congenital malformation of the middle ear	Cleft palate
Genetic syndromes (e.g., Down syndrome, Hunter's syndrome)	Eustachian tube dysfunction

Sensorineural Hearing Impairment	
Congenital viral infections	Meningitis
Maternal rubella	Encephalitis
Cytomegalovirus	Scarlet fever
Prematurity and low birth weight	Measles
Perinatal anoxia or hypoxia	Mumps
Hyperbilirubinemia	Influenza
Rh-factor incompability	Other viral infections
Maldevelopment of inner ear	Cerebrovascular disorders
Hereditary familial hearing impairment (confenital or acquired)	Drug ototoxicity
	Congenital syphilis
Noise-induced hearing loss	Unexplained high fever
Genetic syndromes (e.g., Wardenburg's syndrome, Hunter's syndrome)	Auditory nerve tumors (e.g., neurofibromatosis)

Source: B. Friedrith (1987), Auditory dysfunction. In K. Kavale, J. Forness, & M. Bender (Eds.), *Handbook on learning disabilities, Vol. 1.*

row ear canals and are prone to middle ear infections which may cause hearing impairments. Children or individuals with cleft palates may have repeated middle ear infections which also can result in conductive hearing losses.

Rh (hyperbilirubinemia) can develop incompatibility when a mother who is Rh negative carries a fetus that is Rh positive. The mother's immune system begins to destroy the fetus' red blood cells when they enter the mother's circulatory system. Red blood cells carry oxygen and as a result of this, the fetus may become anemic and die in utero. If the child does survive, he or she is likely to have a high frequency hearing loss. A drug called RhoGam is now available to block the formation of anatibodies in the mother's system. Generally in the first pregnancy the fetus is not affected, but all subsequent ones are if the condition is not identified and treated.

Environmental Causes of Hearing Losses

The environmental effects that begin before birth are associated with illnesses or infections that the mother may have had during pregnancy. For example, a mother who had uncontrolled diabetes may have a child who has a hearing loss.

There is a group of infections that affect the mother and cause serious hearing impairments in the fetus. These infections have been labeled **TORCHS.** The **TO** stands for toxoplasmosis, which is a parasitic disease common in Europe and may be contracted by handling cat feces which is contaminated, or eating infected lamb that has not been cooked sufficiently. The **R** stands for rubella (German measles) which if contracted by the mother during the first three months of pregnancy can cause serious hearing impairments in the child, but also can cause blindness and retardation as well. Now that we have the rubella vaccine, there are not as many cases as in the past. This vaccination must be renewed periodically, though, and many people do not do this. It is also a fact that many children, particularly those who live in the housing tenements of large cities, do not get the rubella vaccine or some of the other vaccines. The **C** stands for cytomegalovirus (CMV), an infection in the mother's uterus which is a major cause of deafness in the United States. CMV often goes undiagnosed and is often misdiagnosed as the flu. A harmful virus can pass through the placenta and affect the fetus. Certain specialists believe that there are some children with hearing impairments that are caused by rubella, but they have not actually been exposed to CMV. CMV is so strongly associated with low birth weight and premature infants, that it has been considered as a possible cause of prematurity as well as the resulting hearing impairments. The **HS** stands for herpes symplex virus which, if left untreated, can lead to serious hearing impairments and can also lead to the death of infected infants. The infants who survive often have serious neurological problems and hearing impairments. There are authorities who believe that CMV is a form of herpes virus.

Loud noises can cause hearing defects. It is suspected by many experts that noises produced by isolettes for premature babies are related to hearing loss, but at this point, this is not conclusive.

There are infections which occur after birth such as meningitis which can damage the auditory nerve.

Otitis media which is a common infection of the middle ear may lead to a hearing impairment. This is particularly true if it is persistent or recurrent and untreated. This otitis media is generally associated with mild to moderate hearing losses.

Asphyxia or a lack of oxygen during the birth process can also cause a hearing loss.

Premature and low birth weight infants are more likely to have hearing loss than infants who are full-term and are not premature.

PREVALENCE

There are about 21 million people in the United States, or 8 percent of the general population, who have some degree of hearing impairments. Most of these hearing impairments are mild to moderate. Only about 1 percent of these people have severe to profound hearing impairments. We have about 68,000 children in the United States who receive special education for their hearing impairments.

The American Speech-Language-Hearing Association has listed several conditions that place an individual in the high-risk category for hearing loss:

1. Family history of childhood hearing impairment
2. Congenital or perinatal infection
3. Anatomic malformations involving the head and neck
4. Birth weight of less than 1,500 grams
5. Bacterial meningitis
6. Severe asphyxia at birth

INTELLIGENCE

Over the past twenty years, there have been reviews of the research concerning the intellectual characteristics of children with hearing impairments. These reviews or research have suggested that the distribution of IQ scores for these individuals is similar to that of hearing children, although the mean IQ score is slightly lower. One study that was conducted revealed that children without hearing impairments scored higher than children who were deaf on three major tests of intellectual development. One striking finding of this study, however, was that the pattern of performance was consistent across the two populations. Children who are deaf, although attaining concepts at a later stage in life, appear to learn them in approximately the same sequence as children with normal hearing.

SPEECH AND LANGUAGE SKILLS

Speech and language skills are the areas of development that are most severely affected for children with hearing impairments. There have been numerous papers published within the past fifty years on just the speech skills of children who are deaf. These publications have clearly suggested that the effects of a hearing impairment on language development vary considerably. For people with mild to moderate hearing loss, the effect on speech and language often is minimal. For individuals with more severe losses, the effect on speech is severe.

EDUCATIONAL ACHIEVEMENT

The educational achievement of students with hearing impairments often is significantly delayed when compared to that of their hearing peers. Children who are hearing impaired have considerable difficulty learning to read and learning the spoken and written language. Low academic achievement is characteristic of students who are considered deaf. They average three to four years below their age-appropriate grade and have problems in social development also. Even students with mild to moderate losses achieve below expectation based on their performance on tests of cognitive ability.

Children with hearing impairments often do better on math than the other subjects. As already stated, reading is the academic area most negatively affected for students with hearing impairments. Spelling performance is also below average for students with hearing impairments, but less than the reading performance. The written language of students who are deaf is simple and limited in comparison to that of their hearing counterparts.

SOCIAL DEVELOPMENT

A child with a hearing impairment modifies the individual's capacity to receive and process auditory stimuli. These children receive a reduced amount of auditory information; therefore, they learn a reduced amount of information. They tend to stay away from hearing children because they do not want their handicap to be discovered. Reviews of the literature on social and psychological development in children who are deaf suggested that these individuals are less socially mature than hearing children.

REFERENCES

Brill, R. B., Mac Neil, B., & Newman, L. R. (1986). Framework for appropriate programs for deaf children. *American Annals of the Deaf, 131*(2), 65–77.

Davis, H. L., & Silverman, S. R. (Eds.). (1978). *Hearing and deafness* (4th ed.). New York: Holt, Rinehart & Winston.

Hallahan, D. P., & Kauffman, J. M. (1991). *Exceptional children.* Englewood Cliffs, NJ: Prentice Hall.

Hardman, M. L., Drew, C. J., Egan, M. W., & Wolf, B. (1993). *Human Exceptionality.* Boston: Allyn & Bacon.

Keller, Helen. (1954). *The story of my life.* New York: Doubleday.

Chapter 8

MILD VISUAL IMPAIRMENTS

Through our visual process, we observe the world around us and develop an appreciation for and an understanding of the physical environment. Vision is one of our most precious sources for the joy of living but most of us take it for granted. From the time we wake up in the morning until we go to bed at night we depend on sight. We rely on our eyes to guide us around our surroundings, inform us through the written word, and give us pleasure, and help us find forms of relaxation.

What if we lost this precious sight or had it impaired? Would our perceptions of the world change? We often think of the severely visually impaired as being helpless and unable to lead a satisfying life.

Visual impairments fall along a continuum with normal vision at one end and blindness at the other. The fewest number of children are found at the extreme end—blindness. According to Barraga (1983),

> a visually handicapped child is one whose visual impairment interferes with his optimal learning and achievement, unless adaptations are made in the methods of presenting learning experiences, the nature of the materials used, and/or in the learning environment. (p. 25)

THE VISUAL PROCESS

The physical components of the visual system include the eye, the visual center in the brain, and the optic nerve, a connection between the eye and the visual center. The basic anatomy of the human eye is presented in Figure 8.1.

The cornea is the external covering of the eye. In the presence of light, it reflects visual stimuli. An opening in the iris is called the pupil which allows the reflected light rays to pass through. The pupil expands or contracts to control the amount of light which enters the eye. The colored portion of the eye is called the iris and consists of membranous tissue and muscles whose function is to adjust the size of the pupil. The lens focuses the light, changing their directions, so that they can fall on the retina. The lens, just like in a camera, reverses the image. The retina

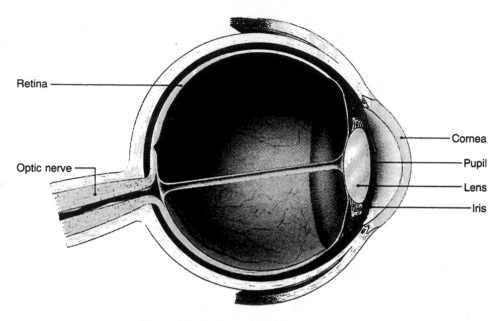

Figure 8.1. Basic anatomy of the human eye.

is the light-sensitive innermost layer of tissue at the back of the eyeball. It contains neural receptors that translate the physical energy of light into the neural energy which results in the experience of seeing. Figure 8.2. shows other structural elements of the eye such as the ciliary muscles, extrinsic muscles, fovea, sclera, aqueous humor and vitreous humor.

The ciliary muscles change the shape of the lens so that the eye can focus on objects at varying distances. Ordinarily, in the mature eye, if it is normal, no muscular effort is necessary to clearly see objects twenty feet or more. When the eye looks at an object less than twenty feet, the ciliary muscles increase the convex curvature of the lens so that the closer object is still focused on the retina. This change in the shape of the lens is called accommodation. The extrinsic muscles control the movement of the eyeball in the socket. This change, made possible by these muscles, is called convergence.

The vitreous humor is filled with a jelly-like fluid which helps to focus light on the retina, while the aqueous humor is filled with fluid between the lens and cornea of the eye. The fovea is a small depression in the shallow pit of the retina at the back of the eye. It contains a great

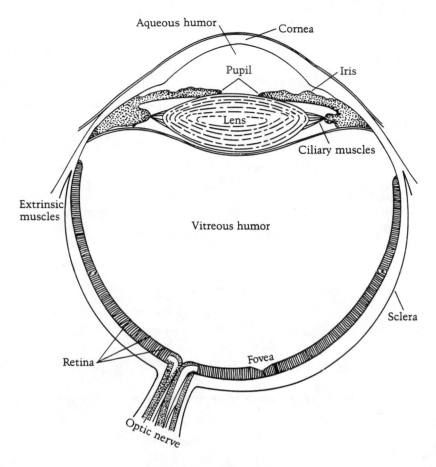

Figure 8.2. The human eye.

number of cones and is therefore the area of greatest acuity of vision: when the eye is directed at an object, the part of the image that is focused on the fovea is the part that is most accurately registered by the brain. The sclera is the white fibrous outer layer of the eyeball.

The optic nerve is responsible for vision. Each nerve contains about one million fibers that receive information from the rod and cone cells of the retina. It passes into the skull behind the eyeball to reach the optic chiasm, the X-shaped structure formed by the two optic nerves, after which the visual pathway continues to the cortex of the occipital lobe of the brain on each side.

DEFINITIONS AND CLASSIFICATION

Definitions

The term visual impairment pertains to people who have a wide range of educational, social, and medical needs directly related to a loss of partial or complete sight. Warren (1989) suggested that visual impairments are associated with people who

> have never had any visual function, those who had normal vision for some years before becoming gradually or suddenly partially or totally blind, those with [disabilities] in addition to the visual loss, those with selective impairments of parts of the visual field, and those with a general degradation of acuity across the visual field. (p. 155)

Legally, a child is blind if he can only see at 20/200 or less, with correction. This means that the child can only see at 20 feet what a person with normal vision can see at 200 feet. The child who is legally blind may be able to sense light and darkness and often has visual imagery. This author has seen legally blind students take the same written test that other students take while functioning in the regular classroom. These same students walk around on campus and other students do not recognize they are blind.

A child who scores between 20/70 and 20/200 on a test of acuity, with correction, is legally partially sighted or has low vision. Some low vision students can read print unassisted by devises while other low vision students need to be assisted by a variety of devises.

A person is also considered legally blind if his or her field of vision is limited at its widest angle to 20 degrees or less. This restricted field is often referred to as tunnel vision, pinhole vision or tubular vision. A restricted visual field will limit one's ability to participate in athletics, drive a car or read.

Levels of impairment are often described in educational terms such as moderate, severe and profound and are not based on acuity but on educational adaptations which are necessary to help these children learn.

CAUSES OF VISUAL IMPAIRMENTS

A wide variety of conditions can cause serious visual problems in children from birth to age 5. Heredity is responsible for 37 percent of the cases of visual problems and is the largest cause.

Table 8.1
Educational Characteristics of Children with Visual Disabilities

Level of Visual Disability	Performance Capability
Moderate	With use of special aids can perform visual tasks like students with normal vision
Severe	Needs more time to perform visual tasks and may be less accurate even with aids and modification
Profound	Performance is difficult in gross visual tasks - detailed tasks may not be handled at all

CLASSIFICATION

Visual impairments may be classified according to the anatomical site of the problem. Anatomical disorders generally include the impairment of the refractive structures of the eye, muscle anomalies in the visual system, and problems of the receptive structures.

Refractive Eye Problems. Refractive problems are the most common type of visual impairments and occur when the refractive structures of the eye fail to focus light properly on the retina. The refractive structures of the eye are the cornea, aqueous humor, lens, and vitreous fluid. The four types of refractive errors are: (1) hyperopia or farsightedness, (2) myopia or nearsightedness, (3) astigmatism or blurred vision, and (4) cataracts.

Farsightedness (hyperopia) occurs when the eyeball is excessively short and focuses the light behind the retina. The person with hyperopia is able to visualize objects at a distance clearly, but unable to see them at close range. This can almost always be corrected by eyeglasses.

Myopia, or nearsightedness, occurs when the eyeball is excessively long which forces the light rays to focus in front of the retina. The person with myopia is able to view objects at close range clearly, but unable to see them from any distance. This condition can almost always be corrected with eyeglasses.

Astigmatism occurs when the surface of the cornea is uneven and this prevents light rays from converging at one point. The rays of light are refracted in different directions and the visual images are unclear. Astigmatism may occur independently of or in conjunction with myopia or hyperopia.

Cataracts occur when the lens become opaque which results in a severely distorted vision or sometimes total blindness. Surgical treatment for cataracts has advanced rapidly in recent years and prevents many serious visual problems.

Muscle Disorders. Muscular defects of the visual system occur when the major muscles within the eye are not developed adequately or athrophic, resulting in a loss of control and inability to maintain tension. The three types of muscle disorders include nystagmus (rapid eye movement), strabismus (crossed eyes), and amblyopia (loss in sharpness of vision).

Nystagmus is an involuntary, continuous, rapid movement of the eyeballs. This movement may be either circular or side to side.

Strabismus occurs when the muscles of the eyes are unable to pull equally; therefore, the eyes cannot focus together on the same object. Internal strabismus occurs when the eyes are pulled inward toward the nose. External strabismus occurs when the eyes are pulled out toward the ears. The eyes can shift on a vertical plane which is, of course, up or down. Strabismus can be corrected through surgical procedures. Children and adults with strabismus often experience double vision. In order to correct the double vision, the brain attempts to suppress the image in one eye. As a result, the unused eye atrophies and loses its ability to see. This condition is called amblyopia. This condition can also be corrected by surgery or by forcing the affected eye into focus by covering the strong eye with a patch.

Receptive Eye Problems. Disorders associated with the receptive structures of the eye occur when there is a degeneration of or damage to the retina or the optic nerve. These disorders include optic atrophy, retinitis pigmentosa, retinal detachment, glocoma, and retinopathy of prematurity. Optic atrophy is a degenerative disease that results from the deterioration of nerve fibers connecting the retina to the brain. Retinitis pigmentosa is a hereditary condition which causes a break in the membrane between the retina and the sclera. The condition appears initially as night blindness, but eventually results in total blindness.

Retinal detachment is caused when the retina is separated from the choroid and the sclera.

Until recently, retinopathy of prematurity was called retrolental fibroplasia. It was one of the most devastating eye disorders in young children. It occurs when too much oxygen is administered to premature infants. Scar tissue forms behind the lens of the eye and prevents light rays from reaching the retina. This condition gained widespread attention in the early forties, with the advent of improved incubators for premature infants. It is still a large cause of blindness throughout the world, but not much of a cause of blindness in America.

PREVALENCE

The prevalence of various visual impairments is often difficult to determine. It would appear that approximately 20 percent of the population has some visual problems, but most of these defects are mild. It is estimated that 1,438,000 people of all ages in the United States have visual impairments that are significant enough to limit their activities. The figure that is most frequently cited for a prevalence figure for school-age children who meet the legal definition of blindness or partial sightedness is 0.1 percent. Based on this percentage, there are approximately 22,960 school-age children with visual impairments severe enough to receive specialized service.

There are thousands of children born blind each year in the United States, but not to the extent that we once had this malady. For example, during the maternal rubella epidemic in 1963 and 1964, a very large number of children were born blind and constituted a large enrollment in special education in residential schools for the blind during the 1970s and 1980s. Maternal rubella is now under control and also retinopathy of prematurity is pretty well under control. However, a large percentage of the cases of blindness still have unknown causes.

Most of the people who are blind in the United States are over the age of 45 years. As a matter of fact, approximately 75 percent of all people who are blind are over the age of 45. This is the reason that this chapter is referred to as people having mild visual defects. There are many children who have mild visual defects who need special adjustments and can get these adjustments in the public school systems. Many of these children will later become blind. However, the emphasis in this chapter is on children who have mild visual handicaps.

CAUSATION

It has already been stated that the largest number of children who have severe visual impairments are that way because of heredity.

Acquired disorders can occur prior to, during, or after birth. These disorders include radiation or the introduction of drugs into the feeding system. A major cause of blindness in the fetus is infection which could be caused by a disease such as rubella or syphilis. It has been estimated that about 14 percent of all cases of legal blindness are caused by infectious diseases. Other diseases which may result in blindness include influenza, mumps, and measles.

Visual impairments which occur after birth are caused by several factors. Accidents, infections, inflammations, and tumors are all a cause of loss of sight. Although the majority of visual impairments occur prior to adolescence or the adult years, approximately 60 percent occur before the age of one. There are some visual problems which occur during adulthood which include injuries, disease, and degeneration.

CHARACTERISTICS

If a child is born with a visual impairment, it will have a more significant effect on his development than one that occurs later in life. It is stated that if a child becomes blind before the age of five, he does not retain useful visual imagery. A child who becomes blind after the age of five has this visual imagery (in the mind's eye) and can imagine things as they look. When a child is totally blind before the age of five, there is a great negative influence on his overall functioning.

INTELLIGENCE

Children with visual impairments are as bright as children who see normally. If a child is born blind, he does not have the experiences of a child who is born with sight. This lack of experiences may cause him to score slightly lower on intelligence tests. However, many studies have confirmed that on tests of intelligence, the performance of individuals with visual impairments may be negatively affected. The only valid way to compare the intellectual capabilities of children who are sighted versus those with severe vision problems is on tasks in which visual impairment does not interfere with performance.

SPEECH AND LANGUAGE SKILLS

Children who are born with severe visual impairments, seem to gain speech at about the same rate as children who are born with sight. There are some differences in language usage and word meaning between the two groups; however, the differences are so small that they do not have a great deal of meaning.

EDUCATIONAL ACHIEVEMENT

The educational achievement of students with visual impairment is often significantly delayed. Some of the variables which influence this delay in educational achievement obviously are in the area of visualization. If the child can't see things, then he can't visualize things. If the child can't see the printed page, his reading will be delayed. Most of these children, though, catch up with seeing children as time goes by, as far as educational achievement is concerned.

SOCIAL DEVELOPMENT

The ability to adapt to the social environment depends on many factors. One of the factors is being able to see. Without vision, perceptions about ourselves and those around us are drastically different.

For most people with a visual impairment, though, these differences in perception do not result in a large problem in social adaptation.

The person who has a vision problem that is significant will have to make many adjustments socially, but these adjustments can be made. This child needs to be introduced to a person who is trained in the education of the visually impaired whether it is in a public school, private school, or institution at a very early age. The teacher or individual who will be working with the child who has a sight problem will be able to help the child as far as social development is concerned. The parents will also be required to help the child as far as socialization is concerned. Social development of visually impaired children is different in several ways from that of sighted children as the factors that produce these differences are complex. All of these factors and obstacles can be overcome.

ORIENTATION AND MOBILITY

A person who has a severe visual impairment may have a severe problem with mobility. The individual may be unable to orient to other people or objects in the environment simply because he or she cannot see them. This person may need the attention of a mobility expert to help him ambulate with the aid of a white cane. He may be given instruction in hand/eye coordination that will help him in such things as eating, brushing his teeth, or even using utensils such as a screwdriver.

PREVENTION

Prevention of visual impairments is one of the major goals among physicians. Prevention measures can be grouped into three categories: (1) genetic counseling, (2) appropriate prenatal care, and (3) early developmental assessment. If these three things are done in an enlightened way, we can prevent many of the causes of blindness. Since many of the causes of blindness are hereditary, it is extremely important for the family to be aware of genetic services. The parents should also be made aware of prenatal care. Adequate prenatal care is a means of preventing problems. Parents must be made aware of the potential hazard associated with poor nutritional habits, the use of drugs, exposure to radiation during pregnancy, etc.

Developmental screening is also a widely recognized means of prevention. Early screening of developmental problems enables the family physician to analyze several treatment alternatives and to refer the child to the appropriate places.

INCLUSION FOR THE VISUALLY IMPAIRED

In 1900, the first public school program for the visually impaired was established in Chicago. These students attended class with their peers for most of the day and received specialized help from a teacher provided by the state's residential school for the blind. This became known as the Chicago model and was adopted by other large cities. During the first half of the twentieth century most visually impaired students received their education from residential schools.

In 1941, there was an alarming increase in the incidence of blindness in premature infants in the U.S. due to retrolental fibroplasia which is now called retinopathy of prematurity. By 1950, U.S. public schools were inundated by the families of children with visual problems who wanted them educated. The residential schools were full. This gave the local schools a large enough student base to have resource rooms with qualified teachers for the visually impaired. Itinerant programs were also started.

Today, less than 15 percent of the visually impaired students are served outside of the regular school program. Most recently, 42 percent of the visually impaired students were served in the regular classrooms. Twenty-three percent received services for less than 60 percent of the school day in a regular class. Across the U.S., residential schools educate only 9 percent of the total numbers of students with visual impairments.

The following is a position statement on several issues about the visually impaired and signed by several organizations from the United States and Canada.

STATEMENT BY THE JOINT ORGANIZATIONAL EFFORT

"Full inclusion," a philosophical concept currently advanced by a number of educators, is not a federal requirement of special education law. Proponents of "full inclusion" nevertheless take the position that all students with disabilities must receive their total instruction in the regular public school classroom regardless of individual needs. Unfortunately, "full inclusion" would eliminate all special placements, including "pull out" services, resource rooms and specialized schools. Such an arrangement would be seriously detrimental to the educational development of many students with disabilities.

We, the national organizations of and for the blind listed below are firmly committed to appropriate educational opportunities designed to provide students with the competencies necessary to ensure full participation in society. It is significant to recognize that our field was the first to develop a broad range of special education options beginning with specialized schools as early as 1829, and extending to public school programs since 1900. These options have provided critically important educational preparation for several generations of highly successful and independent blind people. Based on this long and impressive record of success in making optimal use of both special and public schools programs to meet the diverse needs of blind students, we strongly agree upon the following:

- If provided with timely and adequate specialized services by appropriately certified teachers, students who are blind or visually impaired can develop skills that will enable them to achieve successful and independence as responsible citizens in a fully integrated society. If these students do not receive appropriate instruction designed to develop competencies that meet the sensory deficits of blindness and low vision, critical learning opportunities will be lost, thus diminishing the potential for future accomplishments. In this context, ample opportunities for instruction in such areas as braille, abacus, orientation and mobility, and use of prescribed optical devices must be made available for students, as needed.
- Educational decisions must be made on a case by case basis consistent with the Individuals with Disabilities Education Act (IDEA) which guarantees a Free Appropriate Public Education in the "Least Restrictive Environment (LRE) from among a "Full Continuum of Alternative Placements," based on the Individual Education Plan for each student. Educational decisions

should not be made simply on the basis of philosophy, limited school budgets, administrative convenience, or concerns about socialization.

- Full inclusion in regular education classrooms for all students with disabilities irrespective of individual needs is in sharp conflict with procedural guarantees of IDEA.
- Least Restrictive Environment and Full Continuum of Alternative Placements are critically important IDEA provisions. LRE is not one sole physical location. It is, rather, a principle, which if properly applied, matches the need of the student with an appropriate school setting with meaningful challenges, realistic expectations, and maximum opportunities for achievement and development of healthy self-esteem.
- The regular education classroom may be considered the LRE if the student possesses sufficient readiness and survival skills and can be provided adequate supports, specialized services (from personnel trained in education of the visually impaired), and opportunities to develop skills commensurate with his or her potential. Extreme caution must be exercised so that full inclusion does not result in "full-submersion," social isolation, "lowered" self-esteem, poor performance, or a setting in which services are unavailable.
- In cases where the needs of the student cannot be met in the regular classrooms, an alternative education must be provided and be recognized as the LRE for that particular student. Such alternative placements should not be negatively viewed as discriminatory or as "segregated" settings when legitimately warranted to develop the needed skills for future integration in school and society.
- Since it has been clearly demonstrated that blind children benefit from interacting with disabled and non-disabled children, both interaction opportunities should be encouraged in whatever setting that is considered appropriate. We believe that the mandate in IDEA which states that "to the maximum extent appropriate, children with disabilities [should be] educated with children who are non-disabled," does not intend that blind children avoid interaction with each other.

We strongly urge that decision makers carefully consider and be sensitive to the impact of reform initiatives on the education of students with visual disabilities. Caution must be exercised to insure that educational philosophy and trends such as full inclusion do not seriously endanger appropriate and specialized services for students who are blind or visually impaired. If properly implemented, IDEA can provide legal safeguards to insure that all individual children can realize their full potential for independence and success.

AMERICAN COUNCIL OF THE BLIND
AMERICAN FOUNDATION FOR THE BLIND
ASSOCIATION FOR EDUCATION AND REHABILITATION OF THE
**   BLIND AND VISUALLY IMPAIRED**
BLINDED VETERANS ASSOCIATION
CANADIAN COUNCIL OF THE BLIND

CANADIAN NATIONAL INSTITUTE FOR THE BLIND
NATIONAL FEDERATION OF THE BLIND
NATIONAL LIBRARY SERVICE FOR THE BLIND AND PHYSICALLY
   HANDICAPPED

(From: *Exceptional lives*, Turnbull, A. P., Turnbull, H. R., Shank, M., Leal, D., Merrill/Prentice Hall, Englewood Cliffs, NJ. 1995.

REFERENCES

Barraga, N. (1983). *Visual handicaps and learning* (rev. ed.). Austin, TX: Exceptional Resources.

Warren, D. F. (1989). Implications of visual impairments for child development. In M. C. Wang, M. C. Reynolds, & H. S. Walberg (Eds.). *Handbook of special education: Research and practice.* Vol. 3, Low incidence conditions (pp. 155–172). Oxford, England: Pergamon Press.

Chapter 9

ASSESSMENT OF STUDENTS
FOR SPECIAL EDUCATION

All of us have taken tests during our lives. We were given tests in elementary and secondary schools to measure our scholastic aptitude or intelligence or to measure the extent to which we had profited from experience. We witness today a situation whereby schools are increasingly being held accountable for the performance of their students. It is estimated that pupils attending America's public schools take more than 250 million standardized tests each year.

According to the American Educational Research Association (AERA) and the National Council on Measurement in Education (NCME) a test "may be thought of as a set of tasks or questions intended to elicit particular types of behaviors when presented under standardized conditions and yield scores that have desirable psychometric properties" (1974, p. 2). By testing, we mean that we administer a particular set of questions to an individual or group of individuals in order to obtain a score. Therefore, the score is the end product of testing.

HISTORY OF THE TESTING MOVEMENT

There were very few developments in testing prior to 1879 when a research laboratory was established in Leipzig by Wilhelm Wundt (1832–1920) and became the birthplace of psychological measurement as a scientific field of endeavor.

Wundt and his colleagues laid the groundwork over a hundred years ago in formulating theories of learning which apply to nearly all of the human species. These theories or "laws" are still being debated and expanded today. Recently this area has come under considerable speculation and investigation concerning its potential for early stimulation of high-risk children. According to Gearheart and Willenberg:

The past centennial constitutes some banner years in developing a greater

160

understanding of how and why humans develop, learn, and behave as they do—and the implications of such understandings for educators (1980, p. 5).

An American, James M. Cattell (1860–1944), studied with Wundt at Leipzig and appears to be the first person to use the term "mental test." Cattell and his associates perceived that the measuring of individual differences could have far-reaching effects in the schools and also in industry. Cattell and others had an overwhelming goal of finding a way to assess general intelligence.

Sir Francis Galton (1822–1911) played a very important role in the development of the testing movement. He originated two statistical concepts which caused the psychometric field to flourish. These two concepts were regression to the mean and correlation. These concepts according to Sattler (1989, p. 30) "allowed for the study of intelligence over time, and for the study of the relationship of intelligence test scores between parent and child (as well as other relationships)."

Galton established a psychometric laboratory in 1884. This laboratory was first established at the International Health Exhibition but was later reestablished at University College, London. Sir Francis Galton is regarded by many to be the true father of the testing movement.

In France, Alfred Binet (1857–1911), Victor Henri (1872–1940), and Theodore Simon (1873–1961) developed methods for the study of a variety of mental functions. These investigators discovered the key to the measurement of intelligence and their work was culminated in the publication of the 1905 Binet-Simon Scale. Although the scale was not novel because many of the items had been published in various papers, it can still be considered the first modern intelligence test.

Swanson and Watson stated that the Binet-Simon Test had several unique characteristics:

(1) questions were arranged in a hierarchy of difficulty, (2) levels were established for different ages (establishment of mental age), (3) a quantitative scoring system was applied, and (4) specific instructions for administration were built into the test (1982, p. 9).

The testing movement began to flourish in the United States after the introduction of the Binet-Simon Scale. H. H. Goddard translated the Binet-Simon Scale for use in the United States in 1908. Lewis Terman standardized the Binet-Simon Scale in 1916 and with Maud Merrill revised it in 1937 and 1960.

Terman, in the 1916 translation, increased the length of the test by adding several new items. Terman's revision was called the Stanford-Binet and the original tests were aligned to age levels according to the new norms and the concept of the intelligence quotient was added to the mental age (Swanson & Watson, 1982).

Charles E. Spearman (1863–1945) was an early proponent of a factor analytic approach to intelligence. In 1927, Spearman proposed a two-factor theory of intelligence which stated that a general factor (g) plus one specific factor per test accounts for one's performance on an intelligence test. To Spearman, the g factor was thought of as a general mental energy with complicated mental activities having the highest amount of g. This factor involves the operation of a deductive nature and is linked with a skill. It is also linked with speed, intensity, and extensity of an individual's intellectual output. The cognitive activities associated with g as expressed by Sattler:

> . . . are education of relations (determining the relationship between two or more ideas) and education of correlates (finding a second idea associated with a previously stated one). Any intellectual activity involves both a general factor, which it shared with all other intellectual activities, and a specific factor, which it shares with none (1982, p. 38).

Guilford (1967) conducted some ambitious research relating to intelligence and in the measure of human attributes. Guilford's model (Figure 9.1) includes a cross-classification of attributes with intersecting categories instead of discrete attributes within categories. His model also provides three major categories with subclasses in each. Guilford's theoretical model contains five subclasses of operations, four classes of content and six subclass products for a total of 120 different abilities. According to Swanson and Watson (1983, p. 12), "an intellectual factor in assessing children can result when any one of the five operations combines with any one of the six products and any one of the four contents."

Vernon (1965) notes that many of Guilford's factors of intellect do not show any external validity which could not be accounted for by their general or group values. Eysenck (1967) criticized Guilford's model because it did not reproduce the very essential hierarchical nature of intelligence test data.

A proposal has been made by Arthur Jensen (1970, 1980) that mental abilities fall into two major classes: Level I, which is associative, and Level II, which is cognitive. Rote learning is involved in the associative ability as well as short-term memory. This is measured by tasks which

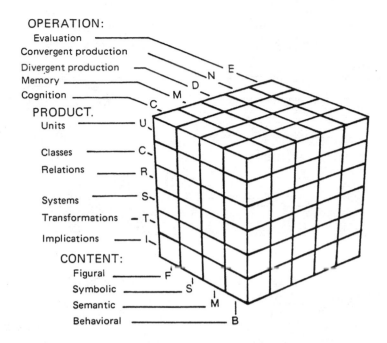

Figure 9.1. Guilford's structure of the intellect model by three dimensions. Source: Guilford, P. *The Nature of Human Intelligence.* New York: McGraw-Hill, 1967, p. 63. Reprinted with permission.

involve digit span memory, free recall, serial learning, and paired-associate learning. In cognitive ability we find reasoning and problem solving and we can measure these by the tests of general intelligence. Most individual general intelligence tests have tasks which involve reasoning, problem solving, use of concepts, verbal and figural analogies, number series, and possibly progressive matrices. Most intelligence tests are likely to measure both of Jensen's levels.

The distinction between level I and II involves a difference in the complexity of the transformation and mental manipulations that occur between the presentation of a given mental task and the response (Sattler, 1982).

David Wechsler (1896–1981) found himself during World War I involved in the large scale intelligence testing program conducted by the U.S. Army. This work so impressed him that he spent the rest of his life engaged in discovering better measurements of intelligence and his work led to major contributions in both theory and practice.

Wechsler received a Ph.D. from Columbia University in 1925 and by 1932 had become chief psychologist at Bellevue Psychiatric Hospital.

Starting in 1934 and continuing to his death he was instrumental in developing intelligence scales which are internationally known: The Wechsler-Bellevue I published in 1939, the Wechsler-Bellevue II or Army Wechsler (1942), the Wechsler Intelligence Scale for Children (1949), the Wechsler Adult Intelligence Scale (1955), the Wechsler Preschool an Primary Scale of Intelligence (1967), the Revision of the Wechsler Intelligence Scale for Children (1974) and the Revision of the Wechsler Adult Intelligence Scale (1981). The Wechsler Intelligence Scale for Children III (WISC–III) in its present form was developed by personnel at the Psychological Corporation. The Wechsler Preschool and Primary Scale of Intelligence (WPPSI) was revised and standardized in 1989 and is now called the WPPSI–R. The WPPSI–R is used with children 3 years through 7 1/4 years.

DIFFERENCES BETWEEN INTELLIGENCE TESTS AND ACHIEVEMENT TESTS

Intelligence tests and achievement tests have likenesses and differences. Humphreys (1971) notes that both types of tests sample aptitude, learning, and achievement and they both sample responses in the child's repertoir at the testing session. The two types of tests also differ in a number of ways. Intelligence tests sample a much wider range of experiences than do achievement tests. Achievement tests are not as valid for measuring learning potential as are intelligence tests. A score on a mathematical subtest of an achievement test, for example, is heavily dependent on formal learning experiences acquired in school. Intelligence tests measure less formal achievement than achievement tests and they also measure the ability to apply information in new ways. Achievement tests stress mastery of factual information such as reading, math, English usage, etc.

PLACEMENT TESTS

These tests note Gearheart and Willenberg (1980) are tests used to determine whether a given student is ready to move into a new unit or a new area of study. These tests are referred to as readiness tests and they might be standardized or teacher-made, but, regardless, the purpose is to determine the degree of readiness or the level at which a child is working. Placement tests are also given to determine if a child is eligible for a special education program. After all requirements for special education have been met, there may be a need for additional assessment to determine which type of program components the child should need. This is called assessment testing.

DIAGNOSTIC TESTS

In diagnostic testing, we evaluate in order to determine specific learning disabilities and provide guidance for individual program planning. In the special education placement process, some diagnostic testing is performed, but it is essential that diagnostic testing take place at periodic intervals during the student's program. Program planning should revolve around diagnostic testing and program modification should come about only after diagnostic testing.

FORMAL STANDARDIZED TESTS

It should be pointed out that formal standardized tests of academic achievement, listening vocabulary, intelligence tests, behavior rating scales, etc. are more important to administrators than to teachers. For example, the formal academic achievement tests enable administrators and subject matter specialists who are responsible for the overall curriculum to judge how students compare in a given district, area, state, or the nation. The tests which are more important for classroom use though are teacher-made tests.

INFORMAL TESTING

To describe an individual performance in basic skill areas, the testing of choice is that developed by the teacher using classroom materials. Informal testing should examine behaviors which the teacher wants the student to demonstrate in daily work; therefore, the teacher should select the test items from texts the student uses in the classroom. In informal testing, the teacher must be able to recognize a random error as opposed to a consistent skill deficit. Because the teacher has the opportunity to base informal testing on the student's work he/she is not likely to mistake a random mistake as a skill deficit. Only those skills which appear to be in deficit need to be tested. The cumulative record will yield the strengths of students in subject matter areas.

Summative evaluation occurs at the end of six weeks or nine weeks and again at the end of the course. This evaluation is typically used to assign grades and is accomplished by criterion-referenced tests as opposed to norm-referenced tests.

A norm-referenced test provides a comparison with some norm group.

In other words, it is a test in which the test results or scores are related to scores for a specific group of students. Often this type of testing leads to grade equivalents, mental age estimates, and so forth.

A criterion-referenced test is one in which the measure of a student's mastery of particular skills in terms of absolute mastery is measured. In this type of testing, we get answers to specific questions such as "Does Susie spell the word *cat* correctly?" Criterion-referenced tests treat the pupil as an individual instead of providing numerical indexes of performance typically expected of others.

The author would like to call attention to Table 9.1 which compares norm-referenced and criterion-referenced tests.

Table 9.1
Comparison of Norm-Referenced Tests and Criterion-Referenced Tests

ADVANTAGES

Norm-Referenced Tests	*Criterion-Referenced Tests*
1. Emphasizes competition with self; deemphasizes competition with others.	1. Reference points are fixed at specified cut-off points and do not depend on a reference group.
2. Helps to determine if a student is achieving up to expectations.	2. Evaluates individual performances in relation to a fixed standard; students competing against self.
3. Evaluates individual performance in comparison to a group of persons; student competing against others.	3. Is content-specific.
4. Designed to maximize variability and produce scores that are normally distributed.	4. Tests are directly referenced to the objectives of instruction.
	5. Identifies those segments of the spectrum of objectives the individual has mastered.

DISADVANTAGES

Norm-Referenced Tests	*Criterion-Referenced Tests*
1. Is vague in relation to the specific instructional content.	1. Many teachers not well equipped to construct such tests.
2. Tests have a low degree of overlap with actual objectives of instruction.	2. Standards may tend to be arbitrary.
3. Generally a poor aid in planning instruction.	3. Cannot measure achievement gains as compared to other children.
4. Tests not sensitive to the effects of instruction.	4. Of little value in identifying the special needs student.

FORMAL TESTS

The following tests are the best and most used individual intelligence tests and they are the most up to date and are appropriate for special education placement.

Wechsler Intelligence Scale for Children— Third Edition (WISC–III)

The Wechsler Intelligence Scale for Children—Third Edition (WISC–III) is an individually administered clinical instrument for assessing the intellectual ability of children ranging in age from 6 years to 16 years, 11 months. The WISC was originally developed in 1949 by David Wechsler and was revised and restandardized in 1974 and again in 1991.

The WISC–III consists of several subtests, each measuring one facet of intelligence. A child's performance is summarized into three composite scores which include: Verbal IQ, Performance IQ, and Full Scale IQ. The standard deviation of the WISC–III is 15 and the mean is 100.

The WISC–III has 13 subtests that are organized into two groups: Verbal subtests and Performance subtests. They are administered in alternating order to keep the child's interest during testing. The reliability of the following subtests are low: Mazes, Picture Arrangement, and Object Assembly.

Verbal Subjects	*Performance Subjects*
2. Information	1. Picture Completion
4. Similarities	3. Coding
6. Arithmetic	5. Picture Arrangement
8. Vocabulary	7. Block Design
10. Comprehension	9. Object Assembly
*12. Digit Span	*11. Symbol Search
	*13. Mazes

Digit Span and Mazes are not used to establish the norms for Verbal and Performance IQ scores and are not needed to obtain these scores. Symbol search can be a substitute for Coding. The child's performance on the 10 subtests produce three composite scores. The sum of the Verbal subtest scores gives the Verbal I.Q. The sum of the Performance subtest scores gives the Performance IQ. The Verbal IQ and Performance IQ are combined (not added or averaged) to furnish the Full Scale IQ score.

In addition to the Verbal, Performance, and Full Scale IQ scores, four factor-based index scores can be calculated. In order to calculate the four factor-based index scores, the subtests of Digit Span and Symbol Search must also be administered.

Factor I (Verbal Comprehension) includes Information, Similarities, Vocabulary, and Comprehension. Factor II (Perceptual Organization) includes Picture Completion, Picture Arrangement, Block Design, and Object Assembly, Factor III (Freedom from Distractibility) includes Arithmetic and Digit Span. Factor IV (Processing Speed) includes Coding and Symbol Search.

The WISC–III is good for a number of purposes. These include psychoeducational assessment as part of the educational planning and placement, diagnosis of exceptionality, clinical and neuropsychological assessment, and research.

The WISC–III is used to diagnose mental deficiencies and it is also used to identify children of high intellectual ability. The WISC–III is able to identify IQs ranging to more than three standard deviations above the mean for a child's age peers. Neuropsychological assessment, which is defined as the study of the brain-behavior relationship, also uses the WISC–III as an integral part of its evaluation. The Wechsler scale is used in neuropsychological tests as part of the evaluations.

The WISC–III is a very complex test to administer, diagnose, and assess. Examiners should have training and experience in the administration and interpretation of standardized, clinical instruments, such as the WISC–R or other Wechsler intelligence scales. The examiner should also have experience in testing children whose ages, linguistic backgrounds, and clinical, cultural, and educational histories are similar to those of the children they will be testing.

The examiner should have completed some formal graduate or professional level training in psychological assessment. A trained technician can administer the subjects and score the response under supervision, the test result should always be interpreted only by an individual with appropriate graduate or professional training in assessment.

Wechsler Preschool and Primary Scale of Intelligence— Revised (WPPSI–R)

The WPPSI–R is an individually administered clinical instrument for assessing the intelligence of children aged 3 years through 7 years, 3 months. The test measures an IQ range of 41–160. The WPPSI–R is a global IQ test and it measures all facets of intelligence. Like its predecessor, the WPPSI, the WPPSI–R provides standardized measures of a variety of abilities thought to reflect different aspects of intelligence. The test is comprised of 12 subtests of which only 10 are needed to determine the IQ.

The first subtest is Object Assembly. This subtest involves giving the child pieces of a puzzle with which they are required to form a meaning-ful whole within a specified time limit. The second subtest is the Information subtest. This subtest requires the child to demonstrate knowledge about events or objects in the environment by pointing to a picture to answer the question. The third subtest, Geometric Design, contains two parts. First the child looks at a simple design and points to one exactly like it distinguishing it from four others. The second part involves the child drawing a geometric figure from a printed mode. The fourth, the Comprehensive subtest, requires the child to express in words his or her understanding of the reasons for actions and the consequences of events. The Block Design, the fifth subtest, requires the child to analyze and reproduce, within a specified time limit, patterns made from flat, one-colored or two-colored blocks. The Arithmetic subtest evaluates quantitative concepts beginning with picture items, then counting tasks, ending with word problems. The seventh subtest, the Maze subtest, requires the child, under time constraints, to solve pencil and paper mazes of increasing difficulty. The Vocabulary subtest has two parts. Beginning with easy picture identification items, then uses verbal definition for orally presented words. The ninth subtest, the Picture Completion subtest, requires the child to identify what is miss-ing from pictures of common objects or events. The Similarities subtest requires a child to pair similar objects, complete a verbally presented sentence that reflects a similarity between two objects, and explain verbally how two presented objects are alike. The eleventh subtest is the Animal Pegs subtest. This subtest is optional and it requires the child to place pegs of the correct colors in holes below a series of pictured animals. Accuracy and speed contribute to the score. The final subtest, the Sentences subtest, is also optional. This subtest involves the examiner reading a sentence aloud and the child repeating it verbatim. A child's performance on these tasks is summarized by a composite score, which serves as an estimate of the individual's capacity to understand and cope with the surrounding world.

The WPPSI–R norms are derived from nine groups of children aged 3 years through 7 years, 3 months, who are considered to be representa-tive of the population of children at these ages in the United States. The WPPSI–R was standardized on a sample of 100 boys and 100 girls in each of the eight age groups, ranging by half years from 3 to 7, and one age group of 50 boys and 50 girls ranging in age from 7 years, 0 months through 7 years, 3 months. The sample was obtained from the four major geographic regions of the continental United States: Northeast, North Central, South, and West. This sample includes the same proportions of Whites, Blacks, Hispanics, and children of other ethnic groups. The parents' level of education and occupation are also used to stratify the sample.

The Wechsler Adult Intelligence Scale—Revised (WAIS–R)

The WAIS–R is the latest edition of an instrument introduced in 1939. In its original version, it was called the Wechsler-Bellvue Intelligence Scale-Form I after David Wechsler and Bellevue Hospital in New York City. A second form of the Wechsler-Bellevue, Form II, was published in 1946. Form I was revised in 1955 and again in 1981. The WISC–R and WPPSI are also derivatives of the 1939 adult scale.

The WAIS–R contains 11 subtests grouped into Verbal and Performance sections. The six Verbal Scale subtests are Information, Digit Span, Vocabulary, Arithmetic, Comprehension, and Similarities; the five Performance Scale subtests are Picture Completion, Picture Arrangement, Block Design, Object Assembly, and Digit Symbol. (Digit Symbol is similar to Coding B on the WISC–R). The WAIS–R covers an age range from 16 years, 0 months to 74 years, 11 months. It overlaps with the WISC–R from 16 years, 0 months to 16 years, 11 months.

The WAIS–R was standardized on 1,880 white and nonwhite Americans equally divided with respect to gender, selected to be representative of the U.S. late adolescent and adult population during the 1970s. The demographic characteristics used to obtain a stratified sample were age, sex, race (white = 1,664, black = 192, and Asians plus native Americans = 24), geographic region (Northeast, North Central, South, and West), education, and urban-rural residence. In the standardization sample, there were nine different age groups (16–17, 18–19, 20–24, 25–34, 35–44, 45–54, 55–64, 65–69, and 70–74), with 160 to 300 individuals in each group.

The WAIS–R, like the WISC–R and the WPPSI, employs the Deviation IQ (M = 100, SD = 15) for the Verbal, Performance, and Full Scales and standard scores for the subtests (M = 10, SD + 3). In order to obtain Deviation IQs, one first converts raw scores into scaled scores, using a table on the front of the WAIS–R record booklet or Table 19 in the WAIS–R manual.

The standard errors of measurement (SE_m) in IQ points, based on the average of the nine age groups, are 2.53 for the Full Scale IQ, 2.74 for the Verbal IQ, and 4.14 for the Performance IQ. Thus, more confidence can be placed in the Full Scale IQ than in either the Verbal or the Performance Scale IQ. The Verbal Scale subtests (average SE_m's range from .61 to 1.24 scaled score points) usually have smaller standard errors of measurement than do the Performance Scale subtests (SE_m's range from .98 to 1.54 scaled score points). Within the Verbal Scale, Vocabulary and Information have the smallest average SE_m's (.61 and .93) scaled score points, respectively); within the Performance Scale, Block Design, and Picture Completion have the smallest average SE_m's (.98 and 1.25 scaled score points, respectively).

The stability of the WAIS–R was assessed by retesting two groups (71 individuals between the ages of 25 and 34 and 48 individuals between the ages of 45 and 54) in the standardization sample after an interval of two to seven weeks. The stability coefficients for ages 25 to 34 were .95 for the Full Scale IQ, .94 for the Verbal IQ, and .89 for the Performance IQ. For the 11 subtests, the stability coefficients ranged from .69 for Picture Arrangement to .93 for Vocabulary. The stability coefficients for ages 45 to 54 were generally similar to those for the younger group. For the three IQs, the stabilities again were high: .96 for the Full Scale IQ, .97 for the Verbal IQ, and .90 for the Performance IQ. Of the 11 subtests, Object Assembly had the lowest stability coefficient ($r_{xx} = .67$) and Information had the highest ($r_{xx} = .94$).

The criterion validity of the WAIS–R has been investigated in a variety of studies by correlating the WAIS–R with the WAIS, WISC–R, Stanford-Binet: Fourth Edition, other intelligence tests, measures of achievement, and years of schooling. Evidence of construct validity has been provided by: (a) the level and pattern of intercorrelations between WAIS–R subtests and scales; (b) the observation that scores on the WAIS–R are distributed in a manner consistent with theoretical expectations; and (c) the results of factor analyses applied to the intercorrelations of the 11 subtests.

The WAIS–R is a highly reliable and valid instrument for measuring the intelligence of individuals between the ages of 16 years, 0 months to 74 years, 11 months.

ACHIEVEMENT TESTS

Peabody Individual Achievement Test (PIAT-R)

The revised edition of the Peabody Individual Achievement Test (PIAT–R) is an individually administered achievement test that assesses six content areas: mathematics, reading recognition, reading comprehension, spelling, general information, and written expression. The PIAT–R is designed for use from kindergarten through the twelfth grade. Although the PIAT–R is a general achievement measure, it also may be used for instructional purposes. Easily administered, the PIAT–R results in a profile of the child's performance in the areas tested. The scores are presented in a variety of forms, including percentile ranks, age and grade equivalents, stanines, and normal curve equivalents. (Written Expression, a new subtest in this version, is scored differently by using scoring criteria provided in the manual.) Depending on the specific evaluation purpose, an examiner may select from these score formats as reporting dictates. Reliability is high for the objectively scored subtests. The manual provides information regarding reliability and validity.

Metropolitan Achievement Test (MAT6)

The sixth edition of the Metropolitan Achievement Test battery (MAT6) is an achievement battery that is group administered. The MAT6 is divided into two groups of tests: the Survey and Diagnostic batteries. The Survey battery assesses students' general achievement in reading, mathematics, language, social studies, and science. The Diagnostic battery addresses the three areas of reading, mathematics, and language. Both batteries are designed for students from about kindergarten through grade 12 (Diagnostic begins at K.5). By design, both the Survey and Diagnostic batteries may be used in norm- and criterion-referenced applications. The Metropolitan is an example of how standardized instrumentation can be designed and used in a meaningful fashion for multiple purposes. Although the normal areas of evaluation are important, equally significant is what can be done with them. When analyzed in terms of the skills required by each item, the MAT6 can provide a vast amount of information about a child's functioning. This information then can be coordinated for specific determination of discrete activities for the child's instructional program. This kind of analysis demands considerable information and teacher training in task analysis and precision teaching. When such educational expertise is brought to the teaching task, instruments like the MAT6 are highly relevant for the education of both children with mental retardation and others.

Key Math—Revised

The Key Math-R is a standardized math test written by Austin J. Connolly, who has a background in education, including a doctorate in education from Colorado State University. The purpose of Key Math-R is to assess a student's comprehension and application of essential mathematical concepts and skills. The Key Math-R is also useful in creating an effective avenue of mathematical instruction for the student. Key Math-R can be given by regular or special education teachers, aides, counselors, school psychologists, and others with psychometric training. Interpretation of the test scores requires knowledge of psychometrics; and, the evaluation can be enhanced if the interpreter is an experienced math teacher.

The Key Math-R was standardized across fourteen states and the sample was representative of grades, sex, socioeconomic level, race, and ethnic background. It was allocated proportionately across geographic regions using children from urban, rural, and suburban areas. One hundred students from each grade were used and two different samples were used: one group was tested in the fall of 1985 and the other in the spring of 1986.

Testing materials include four test easels (each form has two), an individual test record booklet, and a manual. The first easel contains the subtests of the Basic Concepts and Operations content areas. The second easel contains the third content area, Applications. The free-standing easel format serves two main purposes. First, it allows the student to view full-color test plates on one side while, at the same time, the test administrator views presentation and scoring instructions on the other side. Secondly, the easels serve as a shield to prevent the student from seeing the test record.

The Individual Test Record is a twelve-page booklet which allows space for background information about the student, and a summary of scores for each of the four levels of diagnostic information. Space is also provided for profiling scores as well as writing comments and observations which can be used to interpret the student's performance. The test record is designed to allow test scores and student information to be viewed at the same time.

The Key Math-R manual contains six chapters which include directions for administration and scoring of the test and reliability and validity information along with several appendixes.

Wide Range Achievement Test 3 (WRAT-3)

The restandardization of the Wide Range Achievement Test 3 began several years ago. The primary goal of the restandardization was to provide the same level of ease and reliability in usage as previous editions of the WRAT. Also adding and eliminating other items to assure that items for both forms were equivalent. The results are two equivalent test forms that can be administered individually, and used as pre- and post-tests.

The data was compiled during a national stratified sampling involving nearly 5,000 individuals nationwide. The data was analyzed using the Rasch model for item analysis and scaling. As a result, the WRAT-3 continues to be an extremely reliable measurement of the basic academic codes with age norming form a representative sample of individual's codes from all sections of the United States.

The 1993 edition of the WRAT-3 has returned to a single level format for use with all individuals aged 5–75. Two alternate test forms continue to provide the three subtests that have been the strength of all previous editions of the WRAT. Each form takes 15–30 minutes to complete. The length of administration will vary with the skill and behavioral style of the individual being tested.

The three subtests on the BLUE and TAN forms are:

1. *Reading:*   recognizing and naming letters and pronouncing words out of context
2. *Spelling:*   writing name, writing letters and words to dictation
3. *Arithmetic:* counting, reading number symbols, solving oral problems, and performing written computations

The purpose of this test is to measure the codes that are needed to learn the basic skills or reading, spelling, and arithmetic. Absolute scores, standard scores, and grade scores are provided for each of the three subtest areas that can be used to compare the achievement levels of one person to another from kindergarten through adulthood. When used with a test measuring general intelligence that has the same standard deviation units as the WRAT-3, it can be a valuable tool in the determination of learning ability or learning disability.

The three subtests of the WRAT-3 are:

1. *Reading/Word Decoding:*

There are 15 items on the identifying of the alphabet and 42 words for the individual to pronounce. The two parts are to be administered individually. When the individual is eight, the word reading is administered first. When the student has answered five correct response, the points for the letter reading are rewarded. After 10 consecutive missed words, the testing should stop. The individual is given 10 seconds to read the word. In scoring, one point is given for each correct letter and word. A maximum of 57 points can be earned on either the blue or tan form.

2. *Spelling:*

There are 55 items in all. The first 15 items are on name/letter section and 40 items on the spelling section. The name/letter section is for individuals age seven and below or anyone over age eight if they don't spell at least five words correctly on the spelling section. The instructor reads the words and the individual writes them down. This continues until the individual misses 10 consecutive words. The individual is given 15 seconds for each response. In scoring, one point is given for each two correctly written letters in the individual's name as well as each correctly written letter. If letters are reversed, they are regarded as errors. One point is also given for each correctly spelled word. The maximum score of 55 can be earned on either form.

3. *Arithmetic:*

There is a total of 55 items on the arithmetic subtest. The oral section consists of 15 items and the written section has 40 math problems. The oral section is to be given to individuals under 8 or when a teacher does not feel the individual will answer at least five written problems. The written test should be completed in 15 minutes. In scoring, one point is awarded for each oral response and 40 points on the written response. A maximum score of 55 can be earned on either form.

The WRAT–R was nationally standardized in 1992–1993. The item separation indicates how well items define the variable being measured. Of the highest score of 1.00, all nine tests scored .98–.99. Evidence given showed strong evidence for content validity.

ACHIEVEMENT AND INTELLIGENCE TESTS

Kaufman Assessment Battery for Children (K–ABC)

The Kaufman Assessment Battery for Children is an individually administered measure of intelligence and achievement of normal and exceptional children ages 2½ through 12½ years. The Mental Processing Scales measure the child's ability to solve problems sequentially and simultaneously, with emphasis on the process used to produce correct solutions, not on the specific content of the items. In contrast, the K–ABC Achievement Scale focuses on acquired facts and applied skills, therefore, measuring knowledge that a child has gained from the home and school environment.

The K–ABC is intended for psychological and clinical assessment, psychoeducational evaluation of learning disabled and other exceptional children, educational planning placement, minority group assessment, preschool assessment, neuropsychological assessment, and research.

The K–ABC comprises four Global Scales, each yielding standard scores having a mean of 100 and standard deviation of 15. The four global areas of functioning consist of: Sequential Processing, Simultaneous Processing, Mental Processing Composite, and Achievement.

The K–ABC was standardized on 2,000 children, 100 at each half year of age from 2 years, 6 months through 12 years, and 5 months. The sample was stratified on the variables of six, parental education, race or ethnic group (white, black, Hispanic, other), geographic region, community size, and educational placement. The latter variable ensured that the sample would include proportional representation of exceptional children. The standardization procedures were excellent.

The standard errors of measurement vary as a function of the child's age. At the school-age level (eight of 11 age groups), mean values of about 3 points characterize the Achievement Scale; 4 points characterize the Mental Processing Composite, Simultaneous Processing, and Non-verbal Scales; and 5 points are needed for the Sequential Processing Scale. For the Mental Processing subtest, the average values range from about 1 to 1½ points, and for Achievement subtests from about 4 to 6 points. (The Mental Processing and Achievement subtests have different standard score scales, so the numbers are not directly comparable.) When the child's standard score on a scale or subtest is banded by its standard error of measurement, this is interpreted to mean that there is a 68 percent chance that the child's true score falls within this band.

Both split-half and test-retest reliability coefficients, based on the standardization sample, are provided. The split-half coefficients, of the forty-eight age-subtest coefficients, 12 equal or exceed .90. The reliability of the composite Achievement Scale exceeds .90 at all ages. The test-retest coefficients, of the 14 age range-subtests coefficients, 8 equal or exceed .90; the composite Achievement Scale exceeds .90 at the age ranges. Therefore, the composite scales are generally reliable and the subtests are not reliable.

Although there is considerable indication that the battery measures different mental processes, the validity of the battery for the purposes for which it is intended is not established. The manual presents considerable evidence to indicate the K–ABC assesses two different types of mental processing, there is little convincing evidence that the K–ABC can be substituted for more traditional measures of intelligence or achievement. No data are presented to validate the K–ABC as a measure of learning potential, for use in educational placement and planning, for clinical assessment, or for neurological assessment.

The K–ABC is designed to assess the way children process information and the amount of information they have obtained compared to others of similar age and background.

Woodcock-Johnson Psychoeducational Battery—Revised (WJ–R)

The Woodcock-Johnson Psychoeducational Battery-Revised (WJ–R) (Woodcock & Johnson, 1989) is an individually administered, norm-referenced assessment system intended to assess the intellectual and academic development of individuals from preschool through adulthood. Basal and ceiling rules are used so that no subject is administered all of the items. These rules have been changed in the WJ–R. Some criteria are not found in the easel used to present test stimuli. Thus, testers must refer to the examiner's manual during the administration to find the criteria. In addition to the technical manuals that accompany the test, the WJ–R provides four easel kits for presenting stimulus materials: one for the standard cognitive subtests, one for the supplementary cognitive subtests, one for the standard achievement subtests, and one for the supplementary achievement subtests.

The revision represents a substantial modification of the first edition. Some of the new features are ten new tests added to the cognitive battery, four new tests added to the achievement battery, alternate forms for the achievement tests, and the availability of computerized scoring. The tests of interest were dropped from the 1989 edition. The batteries require a skillful examiner to administer and score the subtests (Salvia & Ysseldyke, 1995).

ADAPTIVE BEHAVIOR SCALES

Adaptive behavior is the way individuals adapt themselves to the requirements of their physical and social environment (Schmidt & Salvia, 1984). In part, adaptation means survival: Adaptive behaviors are those that allow individuals to continue to live by avoiding dangers and taking reasonable precautions to ensure their safety. Yet, adaptivity refers to more than mere survival; it implies the ability to thrive in both good and adverse times (Salvia & Ysseldyke, 1995).

In special education, each child must be administered a rating scale for adaptive behavior. Two of the most popular are presented here.

AAMR Adaptive Behavior Scale:
Residential and Community Scale (Second Edition)

The AAMR Adaptive Behavior Scale: Residential and Community Scale, Second Edition (ABS–RC2) (Nihira, Leland, & Lambert, 1993) is an individually administered, norm-referenced scale designed for use with individuals between 18 and 79 years of age. Since its introduction in 1969, this scale has undergone numerous modifications. The latest version has items from previous editions which were selected because of their interrater reliability and effectiveness in discrimination among various levels of adaptation.

The scale is divided into two parts. Part I focuses on ten domains related to independent and responsible functioning, physical development, language development, and socialization. Three factors underlie these domains: Personal Self-Sufficiency, Community Self-Sufficiency, and Personal-Social Responsibility. Two administration formats are used in this part. In the first format, responses to items consist of a series of statements denoting increasingly higher levels of adaptation. These items are scored by circling the highest level of functioning demonstrated by the client. For example, in the domain of physical development, the response to item 25 (vision) has four levels: Has no difficulty seeing; Has some difficulty seeing; Has great difficulty seeing; and Has no vision at all. In the second format, each item consists of a series of statements that are answered either yes or no. A socially desirable response is awarded one point. For example, item 62 (persistence) in the Self-Direction domain consists of five statements: Cannot organize task; Becomes easily discouraged; Fails to carry out tasks; Jumps from one activity to another; and Needs constant encouragement to complete task. For this item, "No" is the socially desirable response; each time a statement does not apply to the subject, the subject is awarded one point. Thus, a subject may receive between 0 and 5 points on this item. Students can earn from 3 to 9 points on each item scored in this format.

The items in Part II of the scale are concerned with maladaptive behaviors that are manifestations of personality and behavior disorders. These items are grouped into eight domains, and only one administration format is used. Two factors underlie these eight domains: Social Adjustment and Personal Adjustment. Each item consists of multiple statements and is scored on a three-point scale (Never 0; Occasionally, 1; or Frequently, 2) (Salvia & Ysseldyke, 1995).

AAMR Adaptive Behavior Scale—2[5]

The revised school version of the AAMR Adaptive Behavior Scale (ABS–S[2]) (Nihira, Leland, & Lambert, 1993) is an individually administered, norm-referenced scale which was designed to be used with children between the ages of 3–21. There are three versions of this scale, 1969, 1974, and 1993.

The items and scoring procedures of the school version of the ABS are identical to those used with the residential and community edition, with two exceptions. On the school version one domain has been deleted from each part to the scale: Domestic Activity from Part I and Sexual Behavior from Part II. Otherwise, the two scales are identical.

Vineland Adaptive Behavior Scale

The Vineland Adaptive Behavior Scale (VABS) is an individually administered scale given by a parent, caregiver, or teacher, who is familiar with the person who is the subject of the assessment. The VABS has been termed the 1984 revision of the Vineland Social Maturity Scale (VSMS). As would be expected, the revision entailed conversion of the old VSMS from an age scale to a much more modern point scale and complete restandardization. The revision is far more sweeping, however; thus, the new VABS might better be considered a new device.

The VABS is available in three forms which have three separate technical manuals. Two forms are termed interview editions: the Expanded Form (Sparrow, Balla, & Cicchetti, 1984a) and the Survey Form (Sparrow,

Balla, & Cicchetti, 1984b). The third form is the Classroom Edition (Harrison, 1985). The three forms vary in the number and types of items included as well as in the respondent who completes the form. The Survey Form contains 297 items and is intended to provide a general appraisal of the individual; it requires about 20 to 60 minutes to administer to a parent or caregiver. The Expanded Form contains 577 items and is intended to provide a comprehensive appraisal suitable for planning educational programs; it requires 60 to 90 minutes to administer to a parent or caregiver. The Classroom Edition contains 244 items and requires about 20 minutes for a teacher to complete.

Individual items form subdomains, and subdomains form domains. All three editions assess Communication, Daily Living Skills, Socialization, and Motor Skills domains. The two interview editions also assess the Maladaptive Behavior domain (Salvia & Ysseldyke, 1995).

REFERENCES

Eysenck, H. J. (1967). Intelligence assessment: A theoretical and experimental approach. *British Journal of Educational Psychology, 37:*81–98.

Gearheart, B. R., & Willenberg, E. P. (1980). *Application of pupil assessment information* (3rd ed.). Denver: Love.

Guilford, P. (1967). *The nature of human intelligence.* New York: McGraw-Hill.

Humphreys, L. G. (1971). Theory of intelligence. In R. Cancro (Ed.) *Intelligence: Genetic and environmental influences.* New York: Grune & Stratton.

Nihira, K., Foster, R., Shellhaas, M., & Leland, H. (1993). *AAMR Adaptive Behavior Scale-School* (2nd ed.). Austin, TX: Pro-Ed.

Salvia, J., & Ysseldyke, J. E. (1995). *Assessment* (6th ed.). Boston: Houghton Mifflin.

Sattler, J. M. (1982). *Assessment of children's intelligence and special abilities* (2nd ed.). Boston: Allyn & Bacon.

Schmidt, M., & Salvia, J. (1984). Adaptive behavior: A conceptual analysis. *Dianostique, 9*(2), 117–125.

Sparrow, S., Balla, D., & Cicchetti, D. (1984a). *Interview edition, expanded form manual, Vineland Adaptive Behavior Scales.* Circle Pines, MN: American Guidance Service.

Sparrow, S., Balla, D., & Cicchetto, D. (1984b). *Interview edition, survey form manual, Vineland Adaptive Behavior Scales.* Circle Pines, MN: American Guidance Service.

Swanson, J. L., & Watson, B. L. (1982). *Educational and psychological assessment of exceptional children: Theories, strategies, and applications.* St. Louis: Mosby.

Vernon, P. E. (1965). Ability factors and environmental influences. *American Psychologist, 20:*723–733.

Woodcock, R. B., & Johnson, M. B. (1989). *Woodcock-Johnson Psychoeducational Battery-Revised.* Allen, TX: DLM.

Chapter 10

PERSPECTIVES ABOUT TODAY'S
STUDENTS AND FAMILIES

Students with exceptionalities do not live in a vacuum. Their exceptionalities are a part of who they are. Therefore, you must gain an understanding of the context of students' lives in order to comprehend the specific impact of exceptionality.

MULTICULTURAL CONSIDERATIONS

Individuals within a family think of themselves as belonging to a family unit. Also, individuals and families think of themselves as belonging to a larger unit—a cultural group. Cultural groups share common beliefs, ways of defining roles and ways of carrying out their responsibilities. The term *culture* refers to the many factors that shape one's sense of group identity: race, ethnicity, religion, geographical location, income status, gender, and occupation.

The U.S. Office of Education, Office of Civil Rights (1987) lists five federally recognized cultural groups in the U.S. They are:

1. *American Indian or Alaskan Native.* A person having descended from any of the original peoples of North America and who maintains cultural identification through tribal affiliation or community recognition.
2. *Asian or Pacific Islander.* A person having descended from any of the original peoples of the Far East, Southeast Asia, the Pacific Islands, including Japan, Korea, the Phillipine Islands, and Samoa.
3. *Latino.* A person of Mexican, Puerto Rican, Cuban, Central or South American, or other Spanish culture or origin—regardless of race.
4. *African-American* (not of Latino origin). A person having descended from any of the African American racial groups of Africa.
5. *White* (not of Latino origin). A person having descended from any of the original peoples of Europe, North Africa, or the Middle East.

The term *multicultural* literally means "many cultures" and refers to the scholar's way of teaching subjects in a way that recognizes the contributions of many cultures in the United States.

The population of the United States is changing rapidly; therefore, multicultural sensitivity and competence is an essential characteristic for being a successful teacher. By the beginning of the twenty-first century, one-third of all school- and college-age students will be from a racial group other than white.

African Americans

The African American population increased 12 percent between 1980 and 1990, reaching close to 30 million persons. African American enroll-ment in the nation's elementary/secondary schools is increased 13 per-cent between 1985–86 and 1994–95, to 6.7 million students.

The number of African Americans among the nation's high school graduates increased 3 percent between 1986 and 1989. Between 1989 and 1995, the number of African American high school graduates de-clined 6 percent. The representation of African Americans in higher education remains well below their representation in the college-age population.

American Indian/Alaskan Native

The American Indian/Alaskan Native population increased 21 per-cent to just under two million persons between 1980 and 1990. In 1990, 64 percent of the American Indian/Alaskan Native population lived west of the Mississippi River. Almost one-half (46 percent) lived in five states (in rank order): Oklahoma, California, Arizona, New Mexico, and Alaska. Enrollments of American Indians/Alaskan Natives in the nation's elementary/secondary schools increased 29 percent between 1985–86 and 1994–95. American Indians/Alaskan Natives are much more likely than other racial/ethnic groups to enroll in two year institu-tions.

Asian/Pacific Islanders

Asians/Pacific Islanders are the fastest-growing population group in the United States. Between 1980 and 1990, the Asian/Pacific Islander population increased 100 percent. By 1994–95, more than 1.6 million Asians/Pacific Islanders were enrolled in the nation's elementary/secondary schools—a 70 percent increase of the number enrolled in 1985–86. In 1989, nearly one-half (49 percent) of all Asian/Pacific Islander high school graduates received their diploma in California or Hawaii. The number of Asians/Pacific Islanders in the 1995 graduating class was

58 percent above the 1986 level. Asians/Pacific Islanders are well represented among postsecondary students.

Latinos

The Latino population in the United States increased 53 percent between 1980 and 1990 and now exceeds 22 million people. The number of Latinos enrolled in elementary/secondary schools increased 54 percent between 1985–86 and 1994–95, from 3.3 million to more than five million students. The number of Latino high school graduates increased 52 percent to more than 213,000 between 1986 and 1995. Nearly 60 percent of the nation's Latino high school graduates are produced by just two states: California and Texas. While Latinos were 12 percent of the 18 to 24 year old population in 1990, in 1988, they made up only 6 percent of all high school graduates, 4 percent of undergraduates in four-year institutions, and 8 percent of students in two-year institutions of post-secondary education.

White/Non-Latinos

White/non-Latinos dropped from 80 percent of the U.S. population in 1980 to 76 percent of the population in 1994. White/non-Latino births increased only 1 percent between 1981 and 1991, compared with 14 percent for African Americans, 31 percent for Latinos, 23 percent for American Indian/Alaskan Natives, and 53 percent for Asians/Pacific Islanders. White/non-Latino enrollment is increasing at a slower rate than any other racial/ethnic group, 5 percent (from 25.8 million to 27 million) between 1985–88 and 1994–95. White/non-Latinos were 78 percent of the 1985 high school graduating class, but are expected to be no more than 22 percent of the 1996 class. White/non-Latinos are represented to a significantly higher degree at all levels of the educational system than would be expected from their representation in the population.

GOOD NEWS ABOUT TODAY'S STUDENTS

The National Center for Education Statistics (1993) has conducted a number of long-term studies on the status and outcome of education. It's *1993 Back to School Forecast* highlighted this good news (U.S. Department of Education, 1992):

1. Preschool and kindergarten enrollment increased by almost a quarter million between 1992 and 1993.
2. The number of high school graduates increased in 1994–95 after dropping during the last 10 years.
3. The number of college graduates were at an all time high in 1993–94.
4. Between 1973 and 1990, the percentage of high school graduates going directly to college increased from 47 percent to 60 percent.
5. After increasing between 1975 and 1985, cocaine use among high school students declined sharply through 1991.
6. While 39 percent of high school students reported in 1979 that they had used illegal drugs in the last 30 days, 16 percent reported such use in 1992.

CHALLENGES OF TODAY'S STUDENTS

The good news, however, accompanies several alarming issues. These issues follow: educational attainment, abuse and neglect, adolescent problems, and children living in out-of-home placements. Students with and without exceptionalities are affected by all of these issues.

Educational Attainment

The Curriculum for Excellence movement tried to improve education by insisting on academic excellence in basic subjects.

The school restructuring movement proposed reshaping the governance and administration of schools.

The comprehensive school movement looked to schools as the source and place of educational, social, health, and other services.

Abuse and Neglect

Physical, emotional, and sexual abuse and neglect of children is on the rise in America. Almost three million children received child protective services for abuse and neglect in 1993, an 8 percent increase over 1992. In fact, the national trend has been a steady growth of child abuse reports since 1985.

There are many reasons why families or other caregivers abuse or neglect children. Some of the factors include the following (Zirpoli, 1990):

1. Care Giver Characteristics. The care giver is a victim of child or spouse abuse or low self-esteem, or experiences a high degree of care giving stress.
2. Environmental Influences. Poverty, family conflicts, unemployment, and substance abuse raise the likelihood of harm.
3. Sociocultural Factors. Our society's acceptance of physical punishment and inadequate child protection services and resources put children at risk.
4. Victim Characteristics. A child's prematurity, difficult temperament, unusual care giving demands, and disabilities endanger the child.

Tragically, physical abuse occurs generally with children under the age of two; emotional and educational neglect rises as children get older. Boys and girls are equally subjected to physical or emotional abuse or neglect, but girls experience more sexual abuse than boys.

Out-of-Home Placement

Many children are taken out of their homes and put into foster care because the courts have found that their parents abuse or neglect them. Sometimes it is found that their parents are incapable of taking care of them for other reasons. About 407,000 children—almost a 50 percent increase between 1987 and 1993—depend on an overused and inadequately staffed foster care system.

Here are some other difficulties:

1. Nearly half of all foster children move from one foster home to another in the same year.
2. Most of them remain in foster care until they are adults and never return to their biological parents' homes.
3. Forty-three percent of these children experience abuse or neglect from their foster families.
4. Although the number of foster care placements has been increasing, the number of qualified foster parents has been decreasing.
5. More states are reporting that children who have been returned to their families are reentering foster care at increasing rates (Children's Defense Fund, 1991; National Commission on Children, 1991a).

EXCEPTIONALITY CONSIDERATIONS

We have learned several things about multicultural considerations and the good as well as the challenging news about today's students. Now we are going to learn some things about exceptionality issues.

TRANSFORMING THE TRADITIONAL PATHOLOGY FOCUS

Traditionists. They are educators and professionals and policy makers who have regarded students with disabilities as being deviant and in need of restrictive and even punitive response from the professional system. These views of deviants and the professional response have varying theories about the nature of the deviants and the most appropriate way to respond to it. If we look at Table 10.1 we will see some of these theories, their emphases and their typical responses.

Table 10.1
Traditional Focus on Children and Youth With Disabilities

Theory	Problem	Typical Responses
Primative	Deviant	Blame, attack, ostracize
Folk Religion	Demonic	Chastise, exorcise, banish
Biophysical	Diseased	Diagnose, drug, hospitalize
Psychoanalytic	Disturbed	Analyze, treat, seclude
Behavioral	Disordered	Assess, condition, time out
Correctional	Delinquency	Adjudicate, punish, incarcerate
Sociological	Deprivation	Study, resocialize, assimilate
Social Work	Dysfunctional	Intake, case-manage, discharge
Regular Education	Disobedience	Reprimand, correct, expel
Special Education	Disabled	Label, remediate, segregate

Table 10.1 underscores the traditional focus on children and youth with disabilities. It is a focus on pathology that has often lead to blaming the victim rather than creating the appropriate and supportive educational opportunities for the growth and development of the exceptional individual.

A long-standing tenet of the field of special education is always "to be realistic." This perspective has given many people a limited but positive vision for the lives of people who have disabilities. In fact, until just recently the majority of professionals in the field of special education would never have believed that certain handicapped people could do the things they have done and could accomplish so much.

VALUES

If the author could choose to teach the reader anything in the book, he would teach this: one should be far more concerned about false despair than false hope. To reinforce this idea, he shares research and best-practice information about people with disabilities. The author hopes that this information will help the reader avoid false despair and create positive visions of what is possible for the handicapped individual when one combines state of the art practices with values.

The first task is to offer a coherent set of values. The six values reject the deviance emphasis, the pathology approach, and false despair in favor of a positive vision that should be a powerful force in the state of the art education. They follow:

1. **Great Expectations.** Students have many capabilities that have not been tapped. We can develop new visions of what is possible for them. These visions can become realities. We need new perspectives of what life can be as well as support for fulfilling these dreams.

2. **Positive Contributions.** The people with disabilities contribute positively to their families, schools, friends, and communities. We need to develop greater opportunities for these contributions.

3. **Inherent Strengths.** Students and their families have many natural capacities. They need greater opportunities for educational programs so they can identify and highlight and build upon their strengths.

4. **Choices.** Students with disabilities and their families can direct their own lives. By enabling them to act on their own preferences, we can allow them to have self-determination.

5. **Relationships.** Connections are crucial to quality of life. Students and their families need to connect to each other and to educators, friends, and their communities.

6. **Citizenship.** Less abled does not mean that any individual is less worthy. Students with handicapping conditions and their families are entitled to full participation in the American way and in American life.

TYPE AND INSTANCE OF EXCEPTIONALITIES

Let us now think about the way schools classify students according to their differences. We find in America that 50.5 percent of special ed students are classified as having specific learning disabilities and they constitute 2,117,087 students. The next largest group of handicapping condition is made up of speech or language impairments, which accounts for 23.4 percent of handicapped children, or 979,207 students. The third largest group in our public schools is mental retardation, which accounts for 12.0 percent of the population of handicapped individuals and constitutes 500,877 students. The fourth largest group of children in the handicapped area are the serious emotional disturbed, which accounts for 8.5 percent of handicapped children classified, or 356,050 students. The next largest group is multiple disabilities, which accounts for 1.9 percent, or 80,272 students. The sixth largest group is the hearing impaired, which accounts for 1.0 percent of the handicapped population, or 42,317 students. Next are the orthopedic impairments, which accounts for 1.0 percent of the handicapped population, or 43,763 students. After that, other health impairments accounts for 1.2 percent of the population, or 52,027 students. In the area of visual impairments, there are 17,783 students, or less than one-half of 1 percent. Finally, the deaf/blind population, with 794 students throughout the United States, accounts for less than 1 percent or really closer to zero percent. Altogether, there are in the United States in the latest figures served in the public schools 4,191,177 students.

What else do we know about these students? According to the most recent Annual Report to Congress from the U.S. Department of Education (1992):

1. The nation's early intervention, preschool and public and private schools were serving just over 4.8 million students in special education in 1994–95.
2. The number and percentage of students receiving special education services have grown annually since Congress passed special education laws in 1976.
3. The number of teachers employed in special education and the number of vacancies that schools could fill if they had qualified teachers available also have grown annually since 1976.
4. The number of students with learning disabilities has more than doubled between 1976–77 and 1993–94. The only other category with any growth was serious emotional disturbance. All other categories decreased in numbers.
5. Males are more likely to be placed into special education than females and males are disproportionately represented in all disability categories.
6. Youth with disabilities also are more likely than the general population of young people to live in single-parent and lower-socioeconomic-status families.

If we continue to look at the make-up of special education students in America, we find that as compared to students without disabilities, students with disabilities are twice as likely to be African American, and only slightly less likely to be white, and are substantially less likely to be Latino. We also find:

1. African Americans are overrepresented in all categories, particularly in the categories of mental retardation and serious emotional disturbance.
2. Latino students are underrepresented in categories of learning

disabilities, mental retardation, and serious emotional disturbance, and overrepresented in health impairments.

3. Wide variability exists in the categorical representation of Latino and American Indian students in different states.
4. Asian/Pacific students are typically overrepresented in the gifted category and under represented in disability categories.
5. White students are consistently over represented in the categories of giftedness and learning disabilities.

The over representation of African Americans has generated intense interest within the field of special education. There is a great deal of concern that centers around the appropriateness of standardized testing for students from culturally diverse backgrounds and the impact of poverty on educational achievement. Some people say the following:

> The reasons for the high disproportion of Black children in special education has been an issue of national concern and debate. Congress . . . suggested that the use of standardized assessment instruments which are racially biased are, at least in part, responsible. Some observers contend that school professionals are more likely to refer and place minority and poor children in special education because of lower expectations regarding the educable ability of these children. Other observers have noted, however, that it is logical to expect a disproportionate number of poor, minority children being placed in special education even if these children are more likely to have experienced poor prenatal and early childhood nutrition and health care, resulting in actual disabilities. (U.S. Department of Education, 1992)

CONCERNS ABOUT CLASSIFICATION AND LABELING

It is impossible to understate concerns of many special educators and families about classification and labeling. On the one hand, classifying and labeling students identifies them in order to provide them with an appropriate education. On the other hand, labeling segregates students with disabilities from their classmates without disabilities, increases the stigma attached to disability, and lowers educators' expectations. Other researchers have noted that many of the discussions concerning the harmful effects of labels have not been sufficiently based on research data. Locust (1988) has this to say:

> Only when formal education came to the Indian Nations were labels supplied to the differences between children. Public Law 94-142, the Education for All Handicapped Children Act (1975), was a two-edged sword for Indian people. On the one hand, it provided educational opportunities for severely disabled children who were once institutionalized off the reservation by the Bureau of Indian

Affairs, but on the other hand, it caused multitudes of children to be labeled mentally retarded or learning disabled who up until that time were not considered handicapped in their cultures.

Some special educators are developing new classification systems that emphasize the student's instructional needs. These educators want to do a better job of distinguishing specific educational approaches, minimizing stigma, and creating opportunity for noncategorical programming.

Labeling

When we have a labeled person that results in some type of action that is taken, often times that label becomes demeaning. Probably the only label that increases a child's self-esteem is the label of giftedness.

SPECIAL EDUCATION OUTCOMES

Special education has made tremendous progress since Congress enacted the 1975 federal special education law, which you have already read about. The major progress has been in providing access to educational opportunities to students with disabilities. The number of special education students has increased every year since 1975 as has their percentage in the total school population. Before the federal law was enacted, students with severe and multiple disabilities, contageous diseases, or aggressive behavior were often excluded from school that now regularly admits all children and youth with disabilities.

EMPLOYMENT

The students who are more likely to have jobs, continue in education and independent living have several characteristics in common. They are:

1. They graduate from high school.
2. They come from a highly educated family.
3. They have no physical impairments.
4. They have good abilities to function and adapt to the mainstream.
5. They are male.
6. They are socially integrated into their community.
7. They do not have a behavior problem.
8. They come from a two-parent household.

The employment rate of recent high school graduates who have been classified as having learning disabilities is similar to the national rate for nondisabled youth, or 62 percent. In spite of these employment estimates, youth with learning disabilities are in positions that are entry level and low paying. Educational experiences are frustrating for children and youth who have learning disabilities. Their dropout rate is high and only 28 percent attempt postsecondary education versus 56 percent for nondisabled youth and most do not have any study skills, reading and math skills, or academic coping skills to successfully get through a four-year college career.

In the area of behavior and emotional disorders, we find that while the employment rate for young adults with behavior or emotional disorders is favorable compared to nondisabled youth it is lower than former students with learning disabilities. For example, students with behavioral and emotional disorders are employed at a 59 percent rate while nondisabled youth are employed at a 62 percent rate. Like their counterparts with learning disabilities, posteducation education participation is low and the dropout rate is high. About 30 percent of these youth are engaged in any productive activity. Nineteen percent live independently.

In the studies we have on mental retardation outcomes, we find the employment rate of young adults with mild retardation is 51 percent and is below the national rate for young adults with no disabilities. We also find that the employment rate falls significantly when severe retardation is considered and only 20 percent of those are employed. Participation in post-secondary education is only one-half to one-third the rate of individuals with learning disabilities and at best one-fourth that of nondisabled youth. Independent living rates are about half that of adults with learning disabilities while rates for living with parents are similar.

IMPACT OF POVERTY

We find that the impact of poverty on families is staggering. As a matter of fact, we find the following:

1. Children are the poorest Americans.
2. One in five children lives in a family with an income below the federal poverty level.
3. Nearly 13 million children live in poverty, with two million more than a decade ago.
4. Many of these children are desperately poor; nearly five million live in families with incomes less than half the federal poverty level.

5. About 44 percent of all African American children and more than 30 percent of Latino children are poor, compared to fewer than 15 percent of white children.
6. Approximately 43 percent of mother-only families are poor, compared to about only 7 percent of two-parent families.

The impact of poverty on families is staggering as has already been stated. Families must try to meet the economic needs of their children and deal with neighborhood violence, drug use, educational problems, and sometimes lack of police protection.

In spite of some very encouraging news about families, many still face many challenges.

SINGLE-PARENT STATUS

The number of children living in single-parent families has risen significantly over the past 20 years. In 1989, 60 million children, or 25 percent of all children, lived in single-parent homes, compared to 12 percent of children in 1970. There are two major causes of single-parenthood: divorce and out of wedlock child bearing. Approximately half of all marriages in the United States end in divorce, which is the highest divorce rate in the world. The National Commission on Children (1991b) tells us that births outside of marriage have increased five-fold since 1960, with about one million babies born each year to unmarried women. Adolescents are particularly likely to have children outside of marriage.

WORK RESPONSIBILITIES

Approximately 11 million children under the age of six have mothers in the work force. Working outside the home creates major time demands on many families. We find that about 50 percent of fathers and 15 percent of mothers report that they regularly work more than 40 hours a week; however, as many as one-third of single parents report that they work over 40 hours a week. About two-thirds of mothers who are not employed report feeling that they have the right amount of time with their families. However, we find that slightly less than one-third of mothers who work 35–40 hours per week report this same perspective. It is obvious that persons who work full time experience greater difficulty in attending school events, participating in conferences with teachers during work hours, and being available for after school care.

GOOD NEWS ABOUT TODAY'S COMMUNITIES

For the future educator, the good news about today's communities is that across the country governors, state and local school officials, professionals and a host of other human service professions, and community leaders are planning to integrate social, health, mental health, and support services in the school. Governor Lawton Childs of Florida has said:

> I look forward to the time when we keep schools open to 10:00 every night, have them going 12 months a year, make them a place where poor families can pick up food stamps and their food from the WIC program (Women-Infants-Children Services) and their AFDC (Child and Family Welfare) checks, and where they can sign up for job training (Center for the Future of Children, 1992).

REFERENCES

Center for the Future of Children. (1992). Staff analysis. *The Future of Children, 2*(1), 6–18.

Children's Defense Fund. (1991). *The state of America's children: 1991.* Washington, DC: Author.

Locust, C. (1988). Wounding the spirit: Discrimination and traditional American Indian belief systems. *Harvard Educational Review, 58*(3), 315–330.

National Center for Education Statistics. (1993). *1993 back-to-school forecast.* Washington, DC: U.S. Department of Education.

National Commission on Children. (1991a). *Beyond rhetoric: A new American agenda for children and families.* Washington, DC: U.S. Government Printing Office.

National Commission on Children. (1991b). *Beyond rhetoric: A new American agenda for children and families—Summary.* Washington, DC: U.S. Government Printing Office.

U.S. Department of Education. (1987). *To assure the free appropriate public education of all children with disabilities: Fourteenth annual report to Congress on the implementation of the Individuals with Disabilities Education Act.* Washington, DC: U.S. Government Printing Office.

U.S. Department of Education. (1992). *To assure the free appropriate public education of all children with disabilities: Fourteenth annual report to Congress on the implementation of the Individuals with Disabilities Education Act.* Washington, DC: U.S. Government Printing Office.

Zirpoli, T.J. (1990). Physical abuse: Are children with disabilities at greater risk? *Intervention in School and Clinic, 26*(1), 6–11.

AUTHOR INDEX

195

SUBJECT INDEX